HOW TO GET WHAT YOU WANT OUT OF LIFE

A step-by-step guide showing how you can make the most effective use of your present and potential capabilities.

HOW TO GET WHAT YOU WANT OUT OF LIFE

REVEALS THE SECRETS OF FINANCIAL, PHYSICAL AND MENTAL WELL-BEING

William J. Reilly

THORSONS PUBLISHING GROUP

First published in the United Kingdom 1983
First published in this format January 1987

*Original American edition published by
Prentice-Hall, Inc., Englewood Cliffs, New Jersey, USA.*

British Library Cataloguing in Publication Data

Reilly, William J.
How to get what you want out of life
1. Self-actualization   2. Self-culture
I. Title
158'.1   BS637.S4

ISBN 0-7225-1406-9

*Published by Thorsons Publishers Limited, Denington Estate,
Wellingborough, Northamptonshire, NN8 2RQ*

*Printed and bound in Great Britain by
Collins, Glasgow*

7 9 10 8 6

THIS BOOK IS AFFECTIONATELY DEDICATED
To My Three Children
ANN, MYRTLE, and NORMAN
Who have played such a large part in
helping me to build my own life

I WISH TO ACKNOWLEDGE

1. The help given me by those who have come to the National Institute for Straight Thinking for counsel on life planning, for they have contributed so much of the factual material upon which this book is based.

2. The creative contributions and the continued editorial improvements made in the preparation of this book by my wife, Gladys Bogue Reilly.

TABLE

OF CONTENTS

Introduction—

WHAT'S IN

THIS BOOK

FOR YOU

THE PURPOSE OF THIS BOOK—WRITTEN FOR MEN AND women of every age group—is to:

1) Help you discover exactly what you want out of life.

2) Give you the courage to go after it.

3) Speed your progress toward a more interesting and creative life.

Psychologists tell us that our main desires revolve around self-preservation, sex, "ego food," bodily comfort, and the use of our five senses. And this is true.

However, different people try to move toward the satisfaction of their basic desires along different paths, to suit their individual tastes.

After all, no two persons are exactly alike. In some respects, *you are different from anyone else who has ever lived or who ever will live.*

Therefore, as an individual, you must arrive at your own *personal* definition of what you want. And this book shows you how to do this.

✡ What Are the Three Magic Mental Attitudes Toward Life?

What happens to a person is not nearly so important as his ATTITUDE toward it.

In Chapter 1 you will be given three magic mental attitudes toward life which, when mastered, will speed your progress enormously, gradually raise you to a new plane of living, and give you a feeling of adequacy and inner security that is well-nigh unshakable.

First, you will be given a *magic mental attitude toward problems* that will make you welcome the problems of life. And after a certain amount of practice in solving your everyday problems for yourself, you will soon enjoy the quiet assurance that *you are equal to the solution of any problem that life can offer.*

Second, you will learn about the *magic mental attitude toward people* that will deepen your understanding of people and that will give you a feeling of spiritual growth and achievement.

Third, you will be given the *magic mental attitude toward yourself* which is absolutely essential if you are to succeed at anything. It will show you the best way to earn the self-esteem that you need in order to be mentally healthy.

✡ Getting Down to Brass Tacks

Now, unfortunately, most people never do arrive at satisfactory solutions to their basic desires because they merely go through the motions of living. They live and die without ever taking the time to think about their purpose in life and what they want out of life.

Because they do not know specifically what they want out of life, they never reach their goal.

Because they do not know exactly where they are going, they run around in circles much of the time or work at cross-purposes—with the result that they never enjoy the thrill of personal growth and achievement that comes from the pursuit of a worthwhile goal.

Obviously, any thoughtful person would like to avoid such an aimless existence.

☼ The Four Main Things Everyone Wants

Using as a general guide the four main things that everybody wants, MONEY, LOVE, "EGO FOOD," and HEALTH, Chapter 2 of this book will set you to thinking about the specific things YOU want under these four main desires, and will help you to arrive at your own personal definition of what you want out of life.

By the time you have finished reading this book, you will readily see how you can:

1) Make the *money* you want with the greatest possible case.

2) Get the *love* you need to be happy.

3) Earn the *self-esteem* and the *admiration of others* that you must have to be mentally healthy.

4) Protect your *health* so that you can really enjoy all the good things of life.

☼ What Are the Three Keys to Growth and Achievement?

Naturally, the more intelligently you act, the more likely you are to succeed at anything you undertake. So in Chapter 3 you will find the three requirements for intelligent action which are also the three keys to all personal growth and achievement.

Your *desire* to do something comes first, for the simple reason that desire is the greatest motivating force in human life. Your *ability* to do it comes second. And your *capacity for handling the human relations involved* comes third.

As we shall see, when you really WANT to do something, half the battle is over—for you are automatically driven to develop your ability to do it and you are just naturally easier to get along with when you are doing what you like to do.

✿ Seven Types of People—What Type Are You?

Most people are as lazy as they dare to be. Most people "get by" making use of only *one* of the three requirements for intelligent action. They fly on only one motor. They are strong on *desire* OR strong on *ability* OR strong in their *human relations*.

Some people have two of these motors running. A few people have all three going strong, and these are the people who really go places.

Since there are only seven possible combinations of these three requirements for intelligent action, we can group various kinds of people into seven types.

But as far as *you* are concerned, the most interesting and most important question is—WHAT TYPE ARE YOU?

When you get into Chapter 3, you will be surprised to see how this method of analyzing people gives you a greater understanding of people in general, while giving you an entirely new understanding of yourself.

When it comes to achieving your life aims, you will find that you never really do "take off" until you get all three motors running.

Chapters 4, 5, and 6 show you exactly how you can do this by:

1) Putting your desires down on paper.
2) Testing your abilities and your human relations to be sure that your desires are *realistic and achievable*.

This self-analysis will reveal—probably for the first time in your life—exactly what makes you tick.

✿ What Are the Three Common Excuses?

When you have finished Chapters 4, 5, and 6, you will know a lot about what you want out of life in terms of MONEY, LOVE, EGO FOOD, and HEALTH.

But you will find in Chapter 7 that knowing what you want doesn't mean a thing UNLESS you DO SOMETHING about it.

To put things off is so easy, especially if you kid yourself with the fallacy that you will be better able to go ahead some time in the future than you are right now.

But when you stall and make excuses for postponing action, you are doomed to stay where you are!

For over twenty years, in confidential sessions with men and women—young, middle-aged, and older—I've been asking people why they do NOT do what they SAY they WANT TO DO, and I haven't heard a new excuse for years.

It's always one or more of three common excuses:

"I haven't the time—right now."

"I haven't the money—maybe next year."

"My folks wouldn't approve."

This Chapter 7 will be especially helpful to you because it will show you how you can free your mind forever of these negative and destructive excuses that keep so many people from doing what they really want to do.

Once your mind is free from these three action-killers, you are ready to move from Part One of this book, in which you've decided what you want out of life, to Part Two, which shows you how to get it.

✡ How to Take That Exciting New Step

Chapter 8 tells you exactly what to do to make your first exciting step successful.

It shows you how to get involved in your new interest right away.

It shows you how to keep your ideas to yourself until they are fully flowered and developed.

It gives you the guts to take your first dive.

It shows you how your first step just naturally leads to your second step and your third step and every step that follows.

In fact, Part Two of this book coaches you, every step of the way, on how to achieve your life desires—one step at a time.

✡ How Straight Thinking Can Speed Your Progress

Everybody has problems.

When you know how to think straight and arrive at sound solutions to your everyday problems, life is a lot more fun and you've got a much better chance of getting what you want out of life than a person who just "muddles through."

Psychologists have been telling us for a good many years now that most people get most of their mental exercise by jumping to conclusions—often WRONG conclusions which only create a lot of NEW problems which never existed before.

In Chapter 9 you are going to see a mind jumping.

You are going to see how we think and how we ought to think.

You will see that there is actually no mystery about the scientific method for solving your everyday problems, and that no matter what kind of problem you bump into —money, job, marriage, divorce, children, in-laws, or what-not—you can make up your mind and be right by following *four simple steps in straight thinking*.

You will learn how to distinguish between what's important and what isn't, so that you don't get all steamed up about something that doesn't amount to a hill of beans.

You will learn how to build balance sheets on important problems so that you can avoid the mental torment of uncertainty and so that you can quickly arrive at a sound decision with a minimum of wear and tear on your mental apparatus.

You will learn how to use the DELAYED RESPONSE to important problems—which is the *first sign of intelligence*.

☼ Are You Having Any Trouble with People?

Now, don't say "No" too fast. For after all, most of our problems are PEOPLE PROBLEMS.

So, in Chapter 10, we give this whole subject a thorough going-over.

It makes no difference what you're after—MONEY, LOVE, EGO FOOD, or HEALTH—you have more fun and fewer worries and it's easier for you to get what you want when people open their minds to you, give you their confidence, and believe in you.

In Chapter 10, you will learn the one sure way to open a closed mind, how to earn a person's confidence, and finally how to deserve a person's belief—which is by all accounts the greatest prize in human relations that life has to offer anyone.

And this is important. For whatever progress you

make toward getting what you want out of life depends largely on those people who have confidence or belief in you—beginning with your mother and ending with your last friend.

✡ *Your Own Personal Design for Achievement*

Finally, in the last chapter of this book, you will see how you can *look ahead* to the years to come and build your own personal design for achievement.

Man or woman, you know that your adult life just naturally divides itself into three parts—the early years, the middle years, and the later years. But in this chapter, you will learn *exactly what this means* in terms of *your life plan from now on.* No matter how old you are *right now,* you will see how the special requirements of your *present situation,* as well as of your future, *can* be met.

However, no matter how great your achievements turn out to be, you must always continue to work toward *even greater accomplishments in the future.*

This is the law of growth.

Here in this chapter you will see designs for men and designs for women—of every age.

Here you will see how you can build your own life planning chart—no matter how old you are and no matter what your goals in life may be.

Here you will see exactly how you can begin to *control* your future from now on—with pleasure and profit.

And here you will see that as long as you entertain bold dreams for the future, you will never grow old.

WILLIAM J. REILLY

PART
ONE

HOW TO DISCOVER
WHAT YOU WANT
OUT OF LIFE

1

THREE MAGIC

MENTAL ATTITUDES

TOWARD LIFE

SOME PEOPLE ARE EASILY UPSET; OTHERS AREN'T.
Some people are squawking about something most of the time; while others, in the same situation, remain calm and collected.

Why?

It's their attitude that makes the difference.

Actually, *what happens to a person is not nearly so important as his attitude toward it.*

No matter what happens to you, there are three magic mental attitudes that will gradually raise you to a new plane of living and give you a feeling of adequacy and inner serenity that is well-nigh unshakable.

1. THE MAGIC MENTAL ATTITUDE
TOWARD PROBLEMS

Life presents a perpetual stream of problems, and that's altogether fortunate, when you stop to think about it. For if you had no problems, no challenges, your life would become very dull and uninteresting. Yet it's amazing how many people "run away" from their problems instead of assuming a "problem-solving" attitude. And thus they deprive themselves of the biggest kick which life has to offer, i.e., "licking a tough situation."

One of the things that impresses me over and over again in my dealings with people is that while it is relatively easy to teach almost anyone the four steps in straight thinking (as covered in Chapter 9), getting a person to USE these four steps in FACING UP TO HIS OWN PROBLEMS is something else again.

Just give us somebody else's problem and we jump to the challenge like a fire horse. But when it comes to our own problem, we're usually not so eager. In fact, we often try to look the other way and pretend the problem isn't there, or we explain it by blaming somebody else, or we run to someone else with it.

Let's be honest with ourselves. Any kind of personal problem makes us feel uncomfortable, and the most natural thing in the world is to try to duck it.

As Bertrand Russell said: "Most people would die sooner than think; in fact, they do so."

And as Winston Churchill observed: "Men occasionally stumble over the truth, but most of them pick themselves up and hurry off as if nothing had happened."

✿ Getting a Problem-Solving Attitude

Your success or failure in anything you might undertake is largely predetermined by whether or not you face up to your problems and assume a "problem-solving" attitude. The sooner we fully realize this, the better.

For example, one night several years ago, I had just settled down in my comfortable chair and adjusted the evening paper in front of my face, when my young son came to me with an arithmetic problem.

"This homework's getting tougher for me all the time," said he.

"Yeah," said I. "But did you ever stop to think—it's *supposed to!* Have you tried this one yourself?"

"Sure—but I haven't the slightest idea how to do it."

"And you want me to show you. Right?"

"Well . . . yeah . . ."

"I'm going to do better than that," I told him. "I'm going to show you how *you* can solve *any* problem you get in arithmetic from now on."

"How do you mean?" He seemed puzzled.

"All you have to do is to look at the problem and say two things to yourself:

>> *First,* this problem can be solved or it
wouldn't be in the book.
>> *Second,* I'm just the guy who can solve
it!' "

With these two thoughts in mind, he went back to his desk and in about fifteen minutes he was at my elbow, proud as punch, with the solution. A simple change in his mental attitude had made the difference.

I am indebted to my mother for giving me this "problem-solving" attitude. One of the earliest recollections of my childhood is that every time I went to my mother with a problem, she would say, "What do *you* think?"

Then she would listen to what I had to say, comment on it, sometimes suggest that I give the matter a little more thought, and usually wind up by complimenting me on my solution.

This gave me plenty of training and plenty of confidence in thinking things through for myself, and I distinctly remember that when I was a sophomore in high school, I finally decided that I was able to handle just about any problem that came up.

☆ How You Can Get Joy and Confidence Out of Problem-solving

Parents can't begin too early to give their children some practice in solving problems for themselves. As Dr. Alan Gregg says, in discussing parents who overload their children with so-called advantages: "They cheat their children of the very thing they are proudest of having done themselves, namely, succeeded in spite of not having had all the advantages." [1]

How true this is! Giving children too much and trying to solve all their problems for them is one of the commonest mistakes made by parents today. I see it so often when parents come to me for help in dealing with the scholastic or career problems of their children in high school or college.

It happened again last week. Elmer G., a distraught father whose son has just finished his second year in college, invited me to lunch. He was all upset because his son wanted to quit school, go into the Army, and finish his college education after he got out.

Elmer told me in considerable detail all he had done for his son, all the advantages he had given him—even

---

[1] Alan Gregg, M.D., "Experiment in Human Heredity," *Wisdom*, June, 1956.

sending him to Europe the summer after his freshman year. Then he told me how he had gone about trying to persuade his son that quitting school was a foolish move. "But my son seems to be fed up with his college studies, and I'm afraid that he might not do so well when we send him back to school this fall. What I want to know is whether you think I'm doing the right thing."

"From what you have told me," I replied, "it seems perfectly clear to me that you have fallen into the natural parental habit of trying to solve all your son's problems for him, instead of giving him the opportunity to solve some of his problems for himself. You're a wonderful person and I can understand why you would like to spare your son all the hardships you had to endure in order to become the successful man you are today. But I would throw this problem of going into the Army right back into your son's lap. Let *him* decide. Once he knows it's HIS decision, he'll do MORE THINKING about it than he ever has up to now. And I might add this. If your son does elect to go into the Army now, it may very well be that two years of Army life right now will give him more maturity than he could get from any educational institution in the world. Furthermore, the scholastic records of those who have been in the service prove that your son will get MORE out of his last two or three years in college *after* he has been in the Army than he would get if he were to finish college now under protest. You're a grand guy but you're doing too much for this boy. You're robbing him of the thrill of achieving things on his own. And I don't know whether you can change or not."

"Well, I can TRY," was his sober reply.

Now I don't know whether *you* have had very much practice in solving *your* problems for yourself or not. But I do know this:

Solving his own problems is a thrilling experience that no one should miss.

Get enough practice at it, and you will eventually feel *equal to the solution of any problem* that life can offer.

This will have an amazing effect on you personally, for you will gradually become a more mature, more productive, and more successful person.

You will *no longer dread* problems. You will actually *welcome them* because you will feel *equal* to them and you will enjoy the exhilaration of solving them.

☼ Making the "Breaks" Fall in Your Favor

"But how about the breaks?" I'm often asked. "Don't you need a certain amount of luck, too?"

Well, I am inclined to agree with Stephen Leacock when he said, "I am a great believer in luck, and I find the harder I work the more I have of it."

Certainly it is possible for us to "make the breaks" in the game of life to a very large extent, so that they fall in our favor. But we would all have to agree that bad breaks do come to innocent people through no fault of their own.

However, I am sure you have often observed that some people are discouraged and defeated when they get bad breaks while others rise above their misfortunes to be bigger and stronger spiritually than they ever were before.

Nearly everyone experiences financial ups and downs, now and then. But as Russell Lynes points out,[1] "A financial depression not only gives people time to think, it *makes* them think. . . . Men and women are not only more ingenious about entertaining themselves, they are more thoughtful about work."

Then he quotes a Milwaukee businessman as saying:

[1] Russell Lynes, "Take Back Your Sable," *Harper's Magazine*, June, 1956.

"My eyeteeth were cut in the depression when I knew people who were going broke and jumping out of windows. I got the habit of living within my income and I have never changed."

✡ How Problem-solving Relieves Tension

But there are bigger problems than financial problems.

We have a neighbor whose first child was born dead. But she didn't cry or worry herself into a nervous breakdown. She faced the facts and said, "We'll try to have another child as soon as possible. And if we can't, we'll adopt one."

In an adjoining town a housewife with four children was stricken with polio, and she is still partially crippled in one arm. But when you talk to her, you'd never know it. For she never mentions it. She's doing a wonderful job of raising her children and running her home. She is one of the most cheerful people I know. Every time I see her I say to myself, "Don't you ever complain about anything again!"

And I know people who have still bigger troubles—and you do too—people with members of their family mentally deficient, mentally ill, blind, or badly crippled for life. But I have observed, just as you have, that these people do a lot less complaining as they go about solving their daily problems than people who have nothing big to complain about.

Fortunately, most people never have to face "big trouble" problems such as these, and I sincerely hope that you never do. But everyone is confronted with some kinds of problems day in and day out. And if you assume a confident "problem-solving" attitude toward the problems you face in your home, in your social life, or on the job, you are certain to gain a lot more self-respect and outside prestige than the person who is always running away from his problems.

Don't be afraid to tackle new problems. Don't be afraid of making a mistake. If you do anything at all, you are bound to make some mistakes. But as long as your batting average is within reason and as long as what you do makes sense, you'll be more often applauded than criticized.

I know of no art, business, trade, or profession that is not hungry for men and women who will take the initiative and go ahead and get the job done instead of having to be wet-nursed every step of the way.

2. THE MAGIC MENTAL ATTITUDE TOWARD PEOPLE

One evening after dinner at my sister's home, when I complimented my young niece, aged eight, for being such a nice girl, she motioned for me to bend over so she could tell me something confidential.

"Do you know why I'm nice to people?" she said softly.

"No—why?" I whispered, wide-eyed.

"Because when you're nice to people, they like you and they give you things," she confided, and giggled.

"That figures!" I nodded.

Yes, it's perfectly natural for us to be nice to the people who help us get what we want out of life. But when it comes to going out of our way to serve perfect strangers, without any prospect of getting anything in return, this calls for a higher degree of maturity. This requires a taste for humanity that usually must be acquired.

☼ Serve Others and Serve Yourself

Once you get into the habit of serving people because they can help you, you soon find that it's a lot of fun and before long—if you try—you'll find yourself gradually assuming a service attitude toward everybody. It's not so much because of what you do *for other people,* although that's important, but what you do *to yourself.*

One of the most beautiful compensations in life is that any time you try to serve someone else, you serve yourself more. It gives you genuine self-respect. It makes you feel great, down deep inside.

For example, some time ago, after a radio interview, I had just returned to my office when a 'phone call came in from a man who had heard the broadcast. The hesitant voice was that of an elderly man who told me in considerable detail about the difficulties he had experienced in his attempt to locate an able secretary.

He talked for three or four minutes and I didn't have a chance to say anything, a state of affairs that always distresses me enormously.

Several times while he was talking, I was tempted to bring him up short and advise him that I do not run an employment agency. But I didn't. I just listened.

Finally he told me that he was staying at a downtown hotel and wanted to know if I could come down to see him that very afternoon.

At that point I was really on the verge of telling him off. But I didn't. I held my fire. And in spite of the fact that I had some other things I wanted to do that afternoon, I decided to be a big man and practice up on my service attitude. So I got into the subway and went down to his hotel to see him.

When I announced myself at the hotel desk, an elderly woman came up and introduced herself. She seemed so pleased that I had come.

"Dr. Reilly, you will never know how much I appreciate your coming down here to see my husband. I want you to meet him."

Then she led the way to a corner of the lobby where he was sitting.

"This is Dr. Reilly, dear," she smiled.

Her husband arose. I put out my hand to reach his. And as he pressed my hand warmly, I found myself looking into the face of a blind man!

I was stunned, and I fairly vibrated with the feeling of gladness that I had come. I shuddered to think that I might have brushed him off over the 'phone.

I spent some time with him and showed him how he could go about getting the kind of secretary he was after.

When I got back to my office, I thanked God for helping me to hold my fire and for sending me downtown to see that man who lives in a world of darkness. I shall never forget this man or the lesson that he taught me.

Yes, a willingness to serve anyone—no matter who he is—whether you get anything out of it or not, is the magic mental attitude toward people. Every great religion and every great religious leader you can think of, stands for this over-all service attitude toward people. If you adopt it, and begin to practice it in your everyday relations with *everyone*, this will have more to do with your spiritual growth and achievement than anything I can think of.

3. THE MAGIC MENTAL ATTITUDE TOWARD YOURSELF

If you stop for a minute and think of the happiest and the most successful people you know, you'll find that all of them have at least one thing in common—*they like themselves.*

Now I don't mean that they have an inflated opinion of themselves or that they are egotistical or that they go around bragging or that they're perfectly satisfied with themselves. What I do mean is that, 'way down deep inside, happy people have a good opinion of themselves. They're not always picking on themselves and condemning themselves. They're not full of a lot of foolish "guilt" complexes. They know themselves and their limitations and they still like themselves—in spite of their imperfections. They've got self-respect.

You show me a person who likes himself, a person who respects himself, and I'll show you a person who has the very first requirement for happiness. You can't hate yourself and still be happy.

☼ Get Into Competition with Yourself

One of the main reasons why so many people get moody and discouraged and wind up with a relatively low estimate of themselves, is that they are always comparing themselves with others who have already achieved outstanding success.

This is a big mistake.

The most important thing is to *get into competition with yourself.*

For instance, when I first went out for the two-mile run on the college track team, the coach gave me a stop watch.

"Just jog around the track today," he told me, "and time yourself. It doesn't make any difference how slow you go to begin with. Tomorrow, jog around a little faster. The important thing is to attempt to improve your time *a little bit* each day."

If, at the outset, the coach had had me run the two

miles alongside a seasoned veteran, I would have been licked before I had really got started.

Don't compare yourself with anyone else. Forget all about the position of others. Measure yourself on your own standards. The only standards are what you have done, what you are doing, and what you can do. You are in a race with yourself and your own possibilities. Where you start or where you stop makes no difference.

✡ The One Essential

The *only essential* is that you PROGRESS SOMEWHERE NEARLY AS FAST AS YOU ARE CAPABLE OF MOVING. Let what you do today compete with and surpass what you did yesterday. Let what you do today measure up to what you are capable of doing.

As long as you do this you will grow, and as long as you feel the exhilaration of achievement and growth, you'll think very well of yourself.

It doesn't make any difference whether you're brilliant, or whether you're highly talented, or whether you're an average person. *It's what you do with what you've got that makes you happy or unhappy.* If you make the most of what you've got, you're happy. If you don't, you're unhappy.

I've seen average people go a lot further than brilliant people because they made the most of what they had. I've seen physically handicapped people do a far better job than those who had both their eyes and arms and legs, simply because they made the most of what they did have.

Just recently, one of the happiest and most successful industrial executives I know told me, "I have so few talents that I just couldn't afford to waste any of them. I've seen brilliant men waste their talents. I never had any to throw away. I'm just an average guy who's had to use everything he's got to get anywhere."

On the other hand, I know a lot of brilliant and talented men and women who are very unhappy because they are able to "get by" without extending themselves at all. And because they never extend themselves, they never experience the satisfaction of growth.

There's no question about it. The best way for you and me to *earn* the self-esteem and self-respect that we need to be mentally healthy is to stop comparing ourselves with other people and go about the business of improving our ability to solve our own problems and extending our service relationships to an ever-widening circle of human beings.

SUMMARIZING THIS CHAPTER

✔ 1. Practice solving your everyday problems for yourself and you'll soon enjoy the quiet assurance that you are equal to the solution of any problem that life can offer.

✔ 2. Be willing to serve anyone—whether you think you'll get anything out of it or not—and you will soon experience a feeling of spiritual growth and achievement that is positively fantastic.

✔ 3. Get into competition with yourself. Let what you do today compete with and surpass what you did yesterday, and you will soon think very well of yourself indeed.

Now let's get down to brass tacks!

2
THE FOUR THINGS
EVERYBODY WANTS

IT WOULD BE RIDICULOUS FOR A PERSON TO GO TO A railroad station and say, "Give me a ticket to the Middle West." Any ticket agent would be understandably puzzled.

"I can't sell you a ticket," he would say, "until you tell me exactly where you want to go. It's got to be Chicago or Peoria or someplace like that."

And yet this is how most people think concerning where they want to go in life. Their destination is entirely too general. No wonder they don't get there!

For years it has been part of my job, as career and business consultant, to ask men and women, "What do you want out of life?"

Few people know.

Unfortunately, most people live and die without ever

arriving at a *specific* definition of their purpose in life.

So the first thing you've got to understand and remember is this: THE MORE SPECIFIC YOU ARE ABOUT WHAT YOU WANT OUT OF LIFE, THE MORE LIKELY YOU ARE TO GET IT.

If you don't know where you want to go, you might land anywhere. And you probably won't like it there. Yet this is what happens to far too many able people.

By the time you have finished the first part of this book, you will know more precisely what you want out of life. And you will have the foundation for a personal philosophy of life that is your very own.

By the time you have finished the second part of this book, you will know how to go about getting whatever you want out of life.

There's really no big secret about the main things everybody wants—in general terms. However, different people move toward the satisfaction of their basic desires along different paths. No two persons are exactly alike. In some respects, YOU ARE DIFFERENT FROM ANYONE ELSE WHO HAS EVER LIVED OR WHO EVER WILL LIVE. As was pointed out in the Introduction, you have your own thoughts, your own dreams, and your own individual capabilities for self-expression. Therefore, as an individual, you must arrive at *your own personal definition* of what you want.

So let's take an introductory look at the four things everybody wants and, in the process, you'll begin to find out how you can be more specific about what satisfies YOU.

☆ 1. You Want Money

To begin with, most people say they want money or something that money will buy. "I've got no problems that a million dollars wouldn't cure," they say.

A junior in engineering school in Pittsburgh can't wait until he gets out of school and lands a good job so he can make some "real dough," pay off his debts, get a new car, and then, maybe, get married.

Florence, a career girl living with her folks on Long Island, wants to make enough money to get a New York apartment of her own and to take some night school courses in personnel administration.

A young Washington, D.C., couple, married for three years, living in a small rooming-house and expecting their first baby, say that their greatest desire is to get enough money ahead so they can put a "down payment" on a little home in the suburbs.

Paul, a middle-aged department store buyer in St. Louis, who feels that he's "giving the boss the best years of my life but I'm not getting anywhere," would like to have enough money to start a business of his own and put his children through college.

A California widow in her forties, with two children in high school, wants enough money to "keep my family together until the children are grown up."

A successful business executive in Boston, who is approaching the retirement age, hasn't saved much money and the company pension he will receive at age sixty-five is rather small. Still he has a high standard of living, and he'd like to have enough money to sustain that standard of living as long as he lives.

As we shall see, most of our "money problems" arise from the fact that we "generalize" too much in our thinking about money.

Most people tell you that they want "more money." But few can tell you exactly HOW MUCH MONEY they want to make this year and in the next five years. And few consciously adjust their financial program, from time to time, to meet changing conditions as life gradually unfolds. Consequently, they don't give enough thought to "what they are going to do" to *get* the amount of money they desire, now and in the future.

If you don't know specifically "how much" money you want, you can get into trouble in two ways—you may not get enough money or you may get too much.

Yes, I said too much. I have seen many a man who just thought he wanted "more money," without knowing "how much" he wanted, lose himself in a race for money only to find that he had lost sight of the other things he wanted that are more important than money.

☼ *2. You Want Love*

Sex drives and undercurrents dominate much of what you do.

Sooner or later most people want to get married. And sooner or later, most people want to have a family.

Obviously, before any marriage can be really successful, there must be, first of all, a strong mutual physical attraction between a man and his wife. Second, there must be a strong mutual mental bond of understanding and common agreement on such vital things as:

> ⇥The sanctity of the home.
> ⇥What constitutes a satisfactory standard of living.
> ⇥The relative importance of money and material things.
> ⇥The philosophy and religion of husband and wife.
> ⇥The right of each individual to live his own life while he enjoys a partnership with others in the home.

If you are married to someone who shares with you the above mental and emotional ties, you've got the kind of love you want—the kind of love that enriches your life.

So many marriages fail because the man and wife are not aware of the requirements of a good marriage in the first place. However, even though we do love and marry the right person, we sometimes lose that love in a preoccupied pursuit of other desires.

Who doesn't know people who have blindly plunged into marriage because they were physically attracted to one another, only to make the belated discovery that they had little in common mentally? And who doesn't know of marriages that have gone on the rocks because the husband spent too little time with his wife and family, or because the wife got too involved in activities outside the home?

✿ 3. You Want Ego Food

Before you can feel reasonably well satisfied, either mentally or emotionally, you must think well of yourself and you must be admired by others.

In a world that has not yet come of age, most people try to get this self-esteem and applause from others by being physically attractive and by acquiring material possessions.

Now I see no harm in wanting good food, stylish clothes, an attractive home, a late model automobile, and many of the modern installations and gadgets that save time or labor. And I can see some health benefits in the desire to be physically attractive and to look good in a bathing suit.

But many who have achieved all this, and many who haven't, have come to realize that there must be a more fundamental way to build a deeper and more satisfying kind of self-esteem and to attain a more genuine and more lasting admiration from others.

Meanwhile, there is a more subtle and more harmful way in which we try to get ego food. We may not be fully aware of it, but we are continually comparing ourselves with others. In these comparisons, we tend to build ourselves up and tear other people down—belittling their appearance, their possessions, their actions, their ideas, or even their achievements, in order to explain away our own failures and insufficiencies.

So many people never seem to outgrow this childish mental attitude toward others. They continue to gloat over the mistakes, minimize the accomplishments, and use the failures and misfortunes of others as the foundation for their own self-esteem.

What a cheap and childish method for trying to gain a feeling of superiority; what a futile way to try to build up one's own ego!

Every thinking person can understand—if he really thinks about it—that his own self-esteem must rest on WHAT HE IS, not on what someone else isn't.

In the long run, what you think of yourself and how much you are admired by others does not depend on what you look like or what you own or on what someone else isn't. It depends on things that run far deeper than these.

Men and career women who like their jobs and who are genuinely interested in and proud of what they're doing, get ego food from their work. Mothers of young children, who realize that they are engaged in the most important job in the world, get ego food from raising a family and making a good home. And all three can get whatever additional ego food they may desire by pursuing their favorite hobbies and by taking an active part in various community activities.

In spite of all this, we have found that most people who work for a living do not enjoy the job satisfaction they should, and are hungry for applause that they never get, while far too many mothers are "bored stiff" just running a home. In later chapters, we'll see what can be done about this.

Even after the breadwinner has reached the retirement age and the mother is finished raising her family, they both still need ego food. And neither can get it by "running out of a reason for existence."

The breadwinner can't get it by retiring and doing nothing and boring the dickens out of everyone by talking about the past. And the mother can't get it by making a nuisance of herself, interfering with the lives of her grown children.

The only way to keep feeding your ego is to continue to follow interesting activities, during the later years, that give you a feeling of self-importance and self-respect as long as you live.

You'll be happier during the later years, you'll feel better, and you'll probably live a lot longer if you find a compelling reason for existence. And in this book, you'll see exactly how it's done.

✡ *4. You Want Health*

Sure, you want health, you'd be the first to agree. You want to survive. The law of self-preservation is the first law of nature.

But let's face it.

Health is the *last* thing many people ever think of until they've lost it. Then, and not until then, do they really appreciate the fact that without good health it is difficult indeed for them to enjoy the other things they want out of life.

I've never felt that you have to be especially smart to take good care of your health *before* you lose it.

Yet nearly every day I see business and professional men endangering their health and their talents with overwork. Without seeming to realize it, they permit themselves to be lured into overworking by a desire for more money than they need and by a desire for recognition or leadership which they've already got.

And it's a great temptation for young people who are just getting started to overload themselves at the expense of their health.

This is what happened to Harold D., who is an ambitious young married man in his late twenties and who works in the accounting department of a San Francisco brokerage house. To get ahead on the job, he was told that he would have to study accounting at night school. Then he made the mistake of scheduling too many courses, with the result that he was averaging only about five hours' sleep at night. His wife could see that he was overdoing things and even some of his friends began to warn him that he was riding for a fall. But it wasn't until he actually collapsed on the job one day and landed in a hospital that he himself arrived at a full realization of the importance of health and the fact that you can't safely undertake two full-time schedules, no matter how ambitious you are.

Good health, for most people, is simply a matter of living sensibly every day. In the long run, how you feel, mentally and physically, largely depends on what happens to you day in and day out—whether you've got the money to pay your bills, whether you enjoy your regular daily activities, whether there is love in the home where you live, and whether you follow sensible everyday habits of eating, sleeping, working, and relaxing.

As Dr. John A. Schindler points out in his best-selling book, *How To Live 365 Days a Year*,[1] which everyone should read:

> Most of the emotionally induced illness we physicians see in our offices does not come as the result of one large terrific emotion, nor even from any series of catastrophes.
>
> Instead, most cases of emotionally induced illness are the result of a monotonous drip, drip of seemingly unimportant yet nevertheless unpleasant emotions, the everyday run of anxieties, fears, discouragements and longings. Clinically, we've known this to be true for years.
>
> When you, or I, or any one of us, has a physical illness, the chances are better than 50 per cent that our illness is emotionally induced.

And what else is there to induce emotional upsets except the problems of getting the four things everybody wants—MONEY, LOVE, EGO FOOD, and HEALTH?

Obviously, all four of these basic desires are intertwined and closely related, and there must be a good balance of all four. To sustain this balance, you've got to be careful that you do not lose sight of one desire while you pursue another.

I'm sure you know people who are pursuing wealth and financial security at the expense of their health or their family life, or those who pursue their sex desires at the expense of self-respect, or those who are chasing fame and a feeling of self-importance at the expense of everything else.

If *you* have a good and well-balanced supply of your own favorite kind of MONEY, LOVE, EGO FOOD, and HEALTH, you're "in business." You are an exceptionally fortunate person. And you feel great. Your chain of happiness is complete. Your main problem is to

---

[1] John A. Schindler, M.D., *How To Live 365 Days a Year*, New York: Prentice-Hall, Inc., 1954.

keep growing and to make your chain even stronger.

However, if one or more of these four links is weak or missing, you don't feel so great. You feel troubled and uncomfortable. What you want is a definite program that will help you to weld the missing links and strengthen the weak ones. And in the following chapters you will learn how to set up such a program for yourself.

JUST REMEMBER THESE MAIN POINTS

✔ 1. The more SPECIFIC you are about what you want out of life, the more likely you are to get it.

✔ 2. You, as an individual, must arrive at your own PERSONAL DEFINITION of what you want.

✔ 3. The four things everybody wants are MONEY, LOVE, EGO FOOD, and HEALTH—all intertwined and closely related. NEVER LOSE SIGHT OF ONE WHILE YOU PURSUE ANOTHER!

3

THE THREE KEYS

TO GROWTH

AND ACHIEVEMENT

We have said that the more *specific* you are about what you want out of life, the more likely you are to achieve it, and that you, as an individual, must arrive at your own personal definition of what you want.

That's true.

But there's more.

Your desires must not only be *specific and personal;* they must be REALISTIC AND ACHIEVABLE—if you are to reach your goals.

Therefore, in Part One of this book, you will not only learn how to *analyze* your basic desires and how to put down on paper in simple sentences exactly what you want out of life; you will also learn how to *test* the validity of your desires and how to find out how *realistic and achievable* they are.

The method of analysis and testing, which has been successfully used by thousands of men and women in practically every walk of life, is based on a fundamental psychological law which has been acclaimed as the most important law of our environment—*The Law of Intelligent Action.*[1]

This law represents a far-reaching contribution to our knowledge of people and what makes them act as they do. And you can use it as an invaluable aid to find out what makes you tick.

In simple terms, the Law says that when you are confronted with any kind of problem, you will *intelligently solve* that problem if you have:

    ➤1 The *desire* to solve it.
    ➤2 The *ability* to solve it.
    ➤3 The capacity for handling the
          human relations involved.

DESIRE, ABILITY, HUMAN RELATIONS: memorize these *key words; remember them!* ALL THREE are necessary to your growth and achievement, no matter what you want out of life.

Now all this seems sensible enough. In fact, you may even have the feeling that you already know this.

BUT DO YOU LIVE BY IT?

Few people do.

Most people just fly on one motor—they are strong on desire OR strong on ability OR strong on human relations.

Some people have two motors running well.

Very few have all three motors going strong.

---

[1] William J. Reilly, *The Law of Intelligent Action,* New York: Harper and Brothers, 1945.

In fact, it is *because* most people *do not* live in accordance with the Law of Intelligent Action that we can group various kinds of people into seven types—since there are only seven possible combinations of the three factors which enter into intelligent action.

SEVEN TYPES OF PEOPLE—WHAT TYPE ARE YOU?

✡ 1. The "D" Type

This type is STRONG on DESIRE; weak on ability and human relations.

Many people fresh from school belong to this type. They would like to set the world on fire, but they are light on experience—ability-wise and people-wise. If they are to succeed, they must graduate from this type. For desire alone, without the ability to back it up and without human understanding, represents a combination which accounts for many of the world's failures.

DESIRE IS THE GREATEST MOTIVATOR IN HUMAN LIFE. When you really WANT to do something, half the battle is over—because you are automatically driven to develop your ability to do it and you are naturally easier to get along with when you are doing what you like to do.

However, we've got to admit that some people have desires that are just plain unrealistic. For example, I am thinking of a young engineer, Karl A., who works in the production plant of a manufacturer of electronic instruments. Karl has made repeated requests to be transferred to the research laboratories of his company. But according to his bosses, Karl simply lacks the analytical and creative ability which they demand of a research scientist.

You undoubtedly know someone who would like to be a great actor or musician or painter or writer or singer, but who lacks the potential ability to reach such a goal.

This gap between the desire pattern and the ability pattern is the source of much unhappiness, that can be corrected only when a person becomes more realistic about what he wants out of life.

I know a contrary bachelor girl who must, for the time being at least, be classified in this type. All she has is the *desire* to get married.

As we all know, the world is full of people who claim they desire to become leaders, or make a lot of money, or do any number of things. But their desires are actually not strong enough to cause them to do anything serious—to develop the required abilities and the required human relations. They just never get past the desire stage. They are dreamers. They are procrastinators.

✵ 2. The "A" Type

This type is STRONG on ABILITY; weak on desire and human relations.

Many genuinely able people belong to this type. The whole trouble with them is that they're "able," but that's about all. They've got brains. They may have highly developed scientific or artistic or administrative or executive ability, but they lack drive or a sense of direction, and they have a talent for insulting people because they are ahead of most people intellectually.

George M., for example, has studied art in Paris and is one of the most creative advertising agency artists in the East. I worked with him a few years ago, and every time I took a client into his office to discuss a magazine advertisement, he wound up arguing with the client. Finally, clients got so fed up, and I did too, that I found another artist who not only had some creative ability but was equal to satisfactory first-hand discussions with the people who had to pay the bills. Obviously, the main thing the matter with George was that he wanted to be a great painter and seemed to resent the fact that he had to work on commercial advertising art, which he often referred to as "corny."

In other words, George had the *ability* to be a great commercial artist. But he lacked the desire. And he was insulting in his human relations.

Tom E. graduated from one of our leading engineering schools and now, in his early thirties, is a brilliant atomic energy researcher in Pittsburgh. His bosses could see that he had a lot on the ball and they tried to push him forward. They put him in charge of a small group of scientists who were working on a special problem. Within a few weeks they could see that they had made a mistake. Tom couldn't get any of these men to cooperate with him. He seemed to antagonize everyone who worked for him because he was so impatient with them —a trait that had not been noticeable when Tom worked alone. The bosses finally had to decide that Tom was miscast as a department head. Now he's working alone again.

I have a good friend who calls himself a "perfectionist" and seems very proud of it. But his marriage is headed for the rocks. He has the ability to make a success of his marriage, but he is forever criticizing his wife for every little thing she does wrong. Consequently, he seems to have lost his desire to make a go of his marriage, has begun to talk about a divorce, and his human relations around the house are abominable. He has yet to learn that THERE ARE NO PERFECT AN-SWERS in our human relations—in the home, on the job, or any place else. And this is perhaps his greatest *IM*perfection. He lacks human understanding.

Yes, many of the most able failures you know belong to this type.

☼ *3. The "HR" Type*

This type is STRONG on HUMAN RELATIONS; weak on desire and ability.

A great many lovable people belong in this class. They are nice people to be around. They seldom enjoy any outstanding success or recognition, but we all prefer them to the "A" type or the "D" type. These people get along with nearly everybody. And they have a genuine service attitude toward people.

For instance, Eddie, who pumps gasoline at a nearby service station, falls into this class. To him, "It's a living." He has no special desire to work at a gas station and he hasn't the ability to work on the engine of your car or do anything of a technical nature or prove to you why you should buy his gas or oil instead of some other brand. But he leaves you with a nice warm feeling inside that makes you want to go back and give him some more business.

Uncounted millions of people hold their jobs and "get by" socially not because they have any special ability or any particular desires in life, but simply because they are friendly and easy to get along with.

Many a young lady has been swept off her feet by a dashing young man who is strong in human relations but who has very little desire to work at anything and no particular ability in any direction. And many a young man has been charmed into marriage by a sociable young lady who has little talent when it comes to running a home or anything else and no particular desire to improve herself.

These three types, then—the D type, the A type, and the HR type—have only one motor running. But you can easily see that *anyone who consciously develops strength in all three directions has three powerful motors working for him and carrying him toward whatever he wants out of life.*

But before we discuss this enviable position of having all three motors running—the "A-D-HR" type—let's take a look at those who have two motors running, which is, after all, better than only one.

☼ 4. The "D-A" Type

This type is STRONG on DESIRE and ABILITY; weak on human relations.

People who belong in this class possess outstanding ability and are fired with a driving ambition to excel. They are "right" an annoyingly high percentage of the time, and they cannot understand why other people are too dumb to do things the right way.

I know an intellectual housewife who has the desire for social success but who is always irritating her family and even her guests with her superior attitude. She has henpecked her husband into the shadows because she has greater mental ability and can find something the matter with nearly everything he ever does or says.

Many of the so-called "experts" belong in this class. I know an efficiency expert who, fired with the desire to be a great leader in the new field of automation, proceeded to make a time-and-motion study which revealed the "one best way" to reduce the number of workers on a production line.

There was only one thing wrong with his plan. The workers who were to carry it out had no say or part in the development of the plan. It was delivered to them complete with orders to follow directions. Consequently, the workers didn't like it. The efficiency expert blew up and the new plan was never used.

It's too bad that so many experts either destroy or limit their usefulness because they are weak or insensitive in their human relations and make little or no effort to think out the human angles.

I know a lawyer, for example, who is a great logician and is motivated by a great desire to win his cases. But he's no good in front of a jury, and has to have someone else plead his case because he feels "above" the use of human appeals which to him seem "trivial."

Actually, people do not like to be "pushed around" by experts, and they don't trust experts whom they don't understand and who make no effort to be understood and accepted.

I know any number of experts who could literally double their income by developing good sound human relations with the people they have to work with.

I'll say this much for experts, though. It might take an expert a long time to admit the importance of human relations. But when he does, at least he has a brain to start with and it doesn't take him too long to change. I've seen some of the most *difficult* experts turn into masters of human relations within a matter of weeks.

☼ 5. The "D-HR" Type

This type is STRONG on DESIRE and HUMAN RELATIONS; weak on ability.

Every art, business, trade, and profession has its share of charming, but impractical dreamers. They are grand people and they have well-developed ambitions and desires, but they just haven't got what it takes to make their dreams come true.

For instance, I had a telephone call from a friend who

is looking for a secretary. He's starting a new business and is enthusiastic about it. But I happen to know he's the D-HR type. Within the past ten years, he's entered into a number of new ventures, and not a single one of them has panned out. Naturally, I'm not too eager to recommend anyone for a secretarial position with him, because I doubt his ability to provide permanent employment.

Business is crowded with naïve enthusiasts who go into business for themselves, who lure others into jobs that do not have a sound future, and who fail.

Unfortunately, many of those who are elected to public office in our democracy fall into this class. When it comes to selecting public servants for important positions in government, it's easy for us to be swept off our feet by the enthusiasm and the personality of a candidate who makes a lot of extravagant campaign promises but who lacks any real ability to make these promises come true.

☆ 6. The "A-HR" Type

This type is STRONG on ABILITY and HUMAN RELATIONS; weak on desire.

These are the able and friendly people who have no particular aim in life and no real purpose that they can get excited about. They have never been inspired to do anything unusual and they have never been frightened into it.

Helen stood at the head of her class in college. And she's one of the most popular young matrons in her town today. But she fritters away her time in a social routine which she admits herself gets pretty dull. When she complained to me about this recently, I asked her, "Well, Helen, what are you looking for in life? What really interests you?" And she came right out and admitted that she had never given any real thought to what she wanted out of life, or what she might be able to get steamed up about.

The playboy son of a successful merchant has a good mind and he has a most attractive personality. But he's been pampered too much by his parents who have tried unsuccessfully to impose upon him their desire that he continue his father's business. He works in the store. But he's not one bit interested in the business. And his parents can't understand why. "It's made to order for him!" they exclaim. "It'll all be *his* some day!"

But that's the whole trouble. There's no real challenge here for him. It's not *his* desire to own the business. And his parents should try to understand that this young man will never reach his full stature until he defines and follows *his own* desires.

☼ 7. The "D-A-HR" Type

This type is STRONG on DESIRE, ABILITY, and HUMAN RELATIONS.

If you ever meet a person who has *all* the required desires, abilities, and human relations to solve *all the problems* of *all kinds of environments* at *all times,* please let me know because you will have met the perfect man —or woman. Of course, we all know there is no such thing—not yet.

At the same time, it is altogether possible for you to

attain the "D-A-HR" status in the work, social, and family environments in which you choose to live.

Among your own friends and associates, you can probably think of at least a few well-balanced and exceptional people who seem to be perfectly adequate most of the time either at home or abroad.

Lincoln approached perfection in the field of government; Sally, the cook at our fraternity house, approached perfection in the kitchen.

Ordinarily, when a person is adequate in his work environment, he tends to run "true to type" in his social or family environment, or vice versa. However, this is not always the case.

I know an accountant who is entirely adequate in his *work* environment, but when he is in a social environment, which includes people with a variety of interests, he's lost.

A man might be a great lover, but a poor provider; a woman might be a leader in civic affairs but inadequate when it comes to training her own children.

Then, too, considering the dimension of *time,* we all change somewhat as the years go by—either for better or for worse. A person who is the D-A-HR type now might become temporarily upset. And as he grows older, he might lose the required desires or the required abilities or the required human relations for one reason or another—unless he makes a conscious effort to keep growing in all three directions.

Now let's turn The Law of Intelligent Action *inward* —let's apply it to ourselves. I, for one, have done this and enjoyed it. And I have shown thousands of others how to do it.

There are so many environments in which I would be completely lost and inadequate: hunting lions, for instance, or even riding horseback.

If you and I went to a circus and a lion happened to

escape in our direction, I would have absolutely no desire to solve this problem, and I won't even discuss my ability or my human relations with lions.

Some time ago, I was inveigled by a group of enthusiasts to go horseback riding on Catalina Island. This was against my better judgment. At the end of the afternoon I felt much disturbed. When dinner time rolled around, I ate my dinner from the mantelpiece.

But it wasn't until I thought of The Law of Intelligent Action that I got to the "seat" of my trouble—lack of ability as a horseman and lack of desire to go horseback riding in the first place. Or in any place, for that matter. Ever since that time I have elected to avoid entirely any horsy environment.

At the outset I could have spared myself a miserable afternoon at horseback riding if I had only asked myself whether I had the necessary desire and ability.

However, for a good many years now, I have been spending an increasing share of my time doing the things *I like to do,* the things *I can do,* and the things that bring me into contact with *people I can get along with.*

After all, every adult is free to select the things he wants to do—to a very great extent. And when you express your own personal preference instead of just going along with the mob, people think more, not less of you. In fact, any mature person knows what he wants and what he doesn't want, in what environments he fits well and in what environments he doesn't, and he can consciously avoid engaging in activities which he fundamentally dislikes.

It's surprising how pleasant and profitable life can be when you're the D-A-HR type. But before you can so classify yourself, there are certain requirements you've got to meet.

Taking your cue from The Law of Intelligent Action,

you will act intelligently, and consequently get what you want out of life when you:

➤➤1 learn your *desires;*
➤➤2 develop the required *ability* to ful-
       fill your desires;
➤➤3 become adequate in your *human
       relations.*

You might even express these three keys to your personal growth and achievement in terms of a simple formula, as follows:

$$D + A + HR = \text{ACHIEVEMENT OF WHAT}$$
$$\text{YOU WANT OUT OF LIFE}$$

SUMMARIZING THIS CHAPTER

To become the D-A-HR type and to get what you want out of life, you must:

✔ 1. Learn specifically what your personal desires are.

✔ 2. Weigh your present and potential abilities to find out whether your desires are REALISTIC and ACHIEV-ABLE—to be sure that you either now have, or can develop in a reasonable length of time, the required abilities to fulfill your desires.

✔ 3. Test your human relations to determine whether they are now adequate and, if not, what you've got to do to make them adequate.

4

THE GREAT

ADVANTAGE OF

PUTTING YOURSELF

DOWN ON PAPER

THE MOST IMPORTANT REASON WHY MOST PEOPLE live and die without ever knowing specifically what they want out of life, is that they never get around to putting their desires down on paper.

Any time you try to put any idea into writing, you're bound to clarify it. In fact, you might even come out with some different idea from the one you started with and you almost always improve your original idea in some way or another.

However, the most significant thing is that once you arrive at a clear definition of what you want, you are much more certain of fulfilling your wishes.

☼ *The Key to a Balanced Life*

While it is true that everybody wants money, love, ego food, and good health, there are as many individual expressions of these four fundamental wants as there are individuals. So if you are really to lead a well-balanced life, it is up to you to get *specific* about your own personal requirements.

Otherwise, you may find yourself pursuing one thing that you want at the expense of another thing that you really want too.

We all know men and women who gradually, almost imperceptibly, undermine their health in the pursuit of money and ego food, and we all can think of men and women who permit their marriage and family relationships to deteriorate through sheer neglect.

In other words, in overreaching for one goal, they lose sight of another!

In fact, it is surprising how many people lead one-sided lives because they have never put down on paper and are therefore not fully aware of what they really want in relation to love, money, ego food, and health. And because they are not fully conscious of what they need to live the full life, they neglect to do the things they should do to enjoy it.

☼ *How You Can Improve Your Present Situation*

You can improve your present situation all right, and as soon as you get specific about what you want, you'll automatically begin to think of *how* you are going to get it. You *can't stop* your mind from thinking along these lines once you give yourself a definite objective.

Actually, you *can control your whole future,* and you are the *only one who can.* But you've got to know specifically what direction you want your future to take and you've got to exert some effort in this direction.

Remember this: EFFORT, WELL-DIRECTED, IS THE FORMULA FOR ACHIEVEMENT.

Happiness and success don't just happen to people; they are thought out and planned for in advance.

The whole trouble is that we are inclined to sit back and "accept our plight" and lazily leave our future to chance, while we hope for some magical "break" to fall our way without any real effort or deliberate planning on our part.

For example, there are many young, middle-aged, and older unmarried men and women who feel the need for love and who would like to get married, but who do little or nothing to expose themselves to likely marriage prospects.

As the only boy in a family of five children, I early became aware of the problems of young ladies who wish to get married. And later, as the father of two daughters, my interest in the subject necessarily became more intense.

One evening, my younger daughter, Myrt, then a sophomore in high school, asked me, "Dad, how can I hook a guy who doesn't even know that I exist?"

And I flippantly told her, without raising my eyes from the newspaper, "I should think that one of the best ways to get a guy to fall for you is to trip him."

And while I am proud to say that all my children have generally followed my sage advice—more or less— I confess that I was somewhat startled the following evening when Myrt rushed up to me and cried, "Daddy! IT WORKED! I tripped him a little and he fell flat on his face! So I helped him up and brushed him off, and Daddy, he asked me for a date for tomorrow night!"

Now I want to clear myself right here and now by saying that I do not approve of what my daughter did —as a general practice. But I do approve of any young lady taking some kind of positive, although perhaps more dignified, action to land the man she wants.

There are plenty of middle-aged and older unmarried men and women, some of them widows or widowers, who would like to get married, if they could meet the right person. I have often counseled such people to get active in local church or political or other community activities, or to take a course of study at some nearby school, or even to take a trip somewhere, or somehow to deliberately circulate and put themselves into contact with good marriageable prospects.

Maybe there are a few highly exceptional people who do live alone and like it, but all the people I have ever gotten to know well and who say this publicly, admit to me privately that they are lonely and do *not* like it and would prefer to be happily married.

✡ *Are You Bored with Your Job?*

Similarly, millions of men and women are dissatisfied with their jobs. But surprisingly few of them make any real effort to define their job preferences and thereby put themselves into an intelligent position to improve their situations. They continue to suffer and go through the motions because they don't take the time to figure out what they really want to do; and even if they do know what they'd prefer as a vocation, they reason themselves into believing that it's "practically impossible to make the switch."

I want to impress upon you right now that *if your job bores you—if it's work, not fun—it's hurting you.* And it's up to you to get out of it as soon as possible and to move into a job you enjoy.

After all, this *business of making a living* intimately and directly *affects all four* of the things that you want out of life: *money, love, ego food, and health.*

Certainly, how a person makes his living determines how much money he makes and how good a provider he is, whether he enjoys the love and respect of his family, how much prestige he enjoys, and whether he thinks well of himself and is admired by others. And, in the long run, how a person makes his living has a whale of a lot to do with his health. As Dr. Thurman B. Rice, Professor of Public Health at Indiana University, says:[1] "The really successful man is the fellow who gets paid for doing the thing he likes to do. He'll not only be happier but the chances are he'll live longer, too. In the Book of Proverbs, it is written: 'A merry heart doeth good like a medicine.' There's no other medicine to be compared with it."

Whenever a person works at a job which he dislikes or is unable to do well, he reflects his inadequacy by being irritable, moody, and nervous. As he continues to feel frustrated, he becomes rebellious, figuratively kicks at people, grows sour on the world. And because he is miscast and cannot be successful in such a job, he fails to make the money he should, he may lose the love and respect of his family or his sweetheart, and he does not think well of himself or enjoy the admiration of his friends and associates.

Yes, it can truly be said that *the person in the wrong job who fails works ever so much harder than the man in the right job who succeeds.*

Now I realize full well that while millions of workers are bored with their jobs, there are also millions of men who are so enthusiastic about their jobs that they seem to have little time for anything else.

Most of these men are married, all right. But they're not working at it.

1 Thurman B. Rice, "Do What You Want—and Live Longer," *Reader's Digest*, November, 1950.

If you are one of these, you too should slow up long enough to put down on paper what you can do about it. For I want to warn you right now that, sooner or later, your life will be seriously out of balance—if it isn't already—unless you give sufficient time and attention to cultivate the continuing love of your wife and your children.

As André Maurois wrote, "A successful marriage is an edifice that must be rebuilt every day."

You are certainly in a well-informed position to figure out what you might do about it if you'll just begin to think about it and record your thoughts.

And don't put it off, as so many busy business and professional men do.

For example, several weeks ago Peter D. told me at luncheon in New York that he was enjoying himself immensely at his job as advertising manager and that for the first time in his life he was satisfied with the amount of money he was making. But when I asked him about his home life, his face clouded up and there was an embarrassing silence. Finally he told me, "I guess that's the one weak spot. In pursuing my career, I seem to have lost touch with my wife and my family."

After we discussed this situation for a while, Peter decided right then and there to take his whole family on his next business trip to the Coast. For after all, his children were having their summer vacation and "going along on a business trip" was something his wife had always yearned to do.

"Another thing," Peter told me, "from now on, I'm going to begin to make a note of things that we might like to do together—as these things occur to me." He looked at me as if he had discovered something that was entirely new to him.

Incidentally, any business or professional man who is all wrapped up in his job needs a "change of pace" to keep from going stale on the job. And I can think of no finer or more rewarding change of pace than spending more time with your family.

There are entirely too many executive, professional, and creative workers who neglect their families and endanger their health and their talents by overwork.

☼ Do You Need To Make More Money?

However, your situation may be quite different.

It may well be that you like your job all right and that you have a well-balanced family life, but you've got to make more money to meet your growing family responsibilities.

There are a great many men who are in this situation and who do a lot of general talking about it without really doing much to boost their income.

For example, Ted K. liked his job as market research director and got a lot of ego food out of it. He's married, has two daughters, and his family life is wonderful. But at forty years of age, he realized that he was in his peak earning years and that he should be making more money if he hoped to see both of his daughters through college and invest some money for the future. However, he never actually did anything about it until I urged him to get *specific* and put down on paper exactly *how much more money* he was after.

As soon as he put down in writing that he needed to increase his income from $20,000 to $30,000 within the next five years, he began to think realistically about HOW he could hope to achieve this increase.

Then, and not until then, did it become perfectly apparent to him—after discussing his situation with his boss—that his company wasn't big enough to pay its market research director very much more than he was now making.

His next step was to talk his situation over with good business friends and sponsors who thought well of him, and within six months he was offered a job as market research director for a much larger company that offered him $22,500. Now, after having been with this company for three years, he's making the $30,000 he was after.

So, getting his money desires down on paper certainly helped Ted to do what was needed to realize his desires. For once he knew specifically what he was after, the other steps just naturally followed.

Now obviously, Ted's money desires may not be the same as yours. Furthermore, it may not be necessary at all for you to change companies to find the opportunity to earn the money you want. But the main idea of setting your financial goal applies, no matter what salary range you're in or what salary range you're after.

Bill D., aged thirty, married for four years, was making $400 a week as a member of the promotion department for a woman's magazine.

But he wanted to begin raising a family and he and his wife felt that they needed more money to do this and to live the way they wanted to. But here again, it wasn't until he put his specific desires down on paper—"to boost my income to around $30,000 a year within the next five years"—and talked the whole thing over with his boss, that he discovered that there were two ways in which he could earn this amount of money within his present company:

▸▸1 He could advance to the job of
      promotion manager, in time.

➡➡2 He could put in a request to become
a regular space salesman for
the magazine.

At first Bill thought that the best way would be to
work toward the promotion manager's job. But when he
fully considered the fact that he would have to come
up with a lot of creative ideas to land and to hold such
a job, he began to doubt whether he was really that
creative. And he began to wonder whether he could
really count on such a plan proving out.

On the other hand, he knew that he didn't have to be
that creative to be a good salesman, and that he could
be more certain of reaching his financial requirements
in this role. Furthermore, as a member of the promotion department of his magazine, he had had contacts
with leading advertisers and he had enjoyed working
with them on their marketing problems.

So Bill put in a request for a salesman's job and about
nine months later there was an opening in the Chicago
territory. He got the job.

Today, Bill is making around $19,000 a year, with the
prospect of making more than the $20,000 which he
originally set for himself.

It seems almost too simple. But it is nonetheless true.
*As soon as you begin to THINK in terms of the SPE-
CIFIC amount of money you're after, you begin to
THINK in terms of SPECIFIC ways to get it.*

So, if you want more money, don't just talk about it.
Don't generalize. Get SPECIFIC. Get it DOWN ON
PAPER. And then you'll be more likely to ACT!

✿ *Housewives Have Their Special Problems*

Every time I talk with a group of men and women
about the great advantage of putting your desires in

writing, I am invariably questioned by at least one woman in the group who says in effect:

"I can see that it's a good idea for men and women who have full-time jobs and maybe even for married women who are forced, by financial circumstances, to contribute to the family income part-time. But I'm a full-time housewife with the job of taking care of my children and running a home, and I don't see any point in my putting a lot of desires down on paper when there's nothing I can do about them."

If you are a full-time homemaker, you too may be inclined to feel that there is no great urgency about putting yourself down on paper—at least right now. After all, your life seems to be pretty well cut out for you for the predictable future, and it may seem that there are not enough hours in the day to do everything now—let alone take on any new projects.

To all this I would certainly agree that since the business of raising a family and running a home is the most important job in the world, it will always take an awful lot of time. But almost in the same breath I also have to tell you that, because your job *is* so important and takes so much of your time, it becomes all the more necessary for you to get some relief and some change of pace through some kind of "other interest."

As Carol K. who recently started to hire a baby sitter on Wednesday afternoons while she works at a local gift shop, told me today, "I really love working there. And now I find that during the rest of the week, little things that would have bothered me around the house, don't."

You know as well as I do that you will do a better job of running a home and raising a family, and you'll be a more interesting person around the house, too, if you do have something else to think about to freshen up your mind and to keep yourself from going stale on the job.

Some outside interest will be good for you—whether you get paid for it or not. Otherwise, you're bound to get into a rut running a home.

So it is important for you, too, to begin to put yourself down on paper by recording some actual ideas concerning what that "other interest" might be.

Another thing, there is no law against your beginning to think about what your main interest is going to be after your children are raised and are able to take care of themselves. For after all, raising a family is not a lifetime job. And after your family is raised, you certainly don't want to make the mistake of trying to continue to live their lives for them, and in the process making a nuisance of yourself.

You want a new and compelling reason for existence. Otherwise, with nothing to do with yourself, you are likely to become a problem and a burden to your children. But a stimulating interest in the later years will give you a new and attractive personality.

We shall see in the next chapter how women who are in the same position as you are now, have succeeded in putting themselves down on paper and have thereby opened the door to a better balanced life immediately.

✻ The Time To Retire Is Never

Even if you're a man who has reached or soon will reach the so-called retirement age, you're not immune to the need for putting yourself down on paper either. For you too need some continuing exciting job interest if you are to enjoy the later years thoroughly. If you try to retire and do nothing, you probably won't even live as long. The old-fashioned idea that a man should make enough money during his peak earning years to retire and do nothing for the rest of his life no longer makes sense—if it ever did.

In the first place, with the present income tax rate, it is virtually impossible for anyone to put aside enough of his earnings to be able to retire at a reasonable age and continue to enjoy the standard of living to which he has become accustomed. Perhaps it was possible to do this some years ago, but as one executive put it, "I'm in the big money now, but I got into big money too late."

In the second place, the whole idea of retirement is psychologically unsound. Whenever any man gets full possession of his time, with nothing to do in it, he usually winds up playing too much, or drinking too much, or smoking too much, or loafing too much, or talking too much about the things he used to do in the good old days. He misses the prestige which goes with an important position.

As one retired executive complained in a *New York Times* advertisement, "I am tired of golf and play, and North and South resorts, and I find my efforts at 'do-gooding' do not keep me keen and interested. I wish again to work, and work hard . . ."

We have found only one satisfactory solution to this problem. The time to retire is NEVER.

In order to continue to enjoy the income and the prestige and the growth provided by an exciting job interest in the later years, the successful person must set up his own business or other activity which he owns, lock, stock, and barrel, and over which he exercises complete CONTROL so that no one can fire him.

✪ And Don't Forget About Your Health

If you're sick, I don't have to tell you to do something about it. For when "it hurts you right here" you finally do something about it without anybody telling you.

But most people aren't sick—yet. It's just that they have permitted themselves to fall into habits of immoderation that finally catch up to them and make them sick.

One of the first pieces of prose that ever made an impression on me is: "Man tends to eliminate his sources of pleasure, one by one, through excesses, until at last there are only a few left and these are so strong that they kill him."

So if you smoke too much or drink too much or work too much or eat too much or weigh too much or sleep too little, it's entirely your own fault and you know it, of course.

But just *knowing* this isn't going to change anything. It's what you DO about it that counts.

And you're not going to DO anything about it until you begin to THINK about it.

However, one of the toughest jobs in the world is to get anyone to think about his health UNTIL HE LOSES IT. The easiest way in the world to begin thinking about your health before you lose it is to put your bad habits down on paper and make a note of what YOU'RE GOING TO DO about them. After all, there's something about putting "what you're going to do about it" on paper that gets under your skin and needles you into doing what you said you were going to do.

✿ Get Yourself a Notebook

So no matter who you are or what your present situation may be, it's a great advantage to you to put your desires down on paper—NOW. For if you don't, your mind will simply continue to flit from one wish to another and you may never come to any firm conclusions at all. You may never know exactly what you want out of life in terms of money, love, ego food, and health, and consequently you stand a poor chance of getting it.

In the next chapter, you will see how others have suc-

ceeded in putting their personal desires down on paper.
But before you turn to this chapter, get yourself a notebook so that you can begin to record the thoughts
concerning YOUR personal desires that will certainly
come to your mind as you read.

You might use a loose-leaf notebook, or, if you prefer,
a stenographer's notebook.

In any case, you will find, as you fill the pages of this
notebook, that you are beginning to write a fascinating
life character-story about a person you are very fond
of—YOU.

This story, as it unfolds, will help you to know yourself a little better, and it won't be very many days until
you will know a lot about what you *really* want out of
life. And what's more, you will find that you are beginning to figure out ways of getting it.

SUMMARY OF THIS CHAPTER

✔ 1. The most important reason why most people live and
die without knowing specifically what they want out
of life is that they never get around to putting their
desires into writing.

✔ 2. Once you arrive at a clear definition of what you
want, your wishes are much more likely to come true.

✔ 3. Without a clear definition of your desires, you are
likely to pursue one thing you want at the expense of
another thing you really want too.

✔ 4. Get yourself a notebook and begin to record your
thoughts as you read the next chapter.

5 HOW TO DEFINE YOUR PERSONAL DESIRES

I KNOW OF NO BETTER WAY TO PREDICT ANY PERson's future than to plumb the depths of his real desires.

This is the dominant reason why everyone should give himself a chance to explore his inner desires.

It may well be that you are an exceptional person and that you already know exactly what you want out of life in terms of money, love, ego food, and health. You may have picked up this book wanting only to know how to get what you want a little faster and a little easier.

However, most readers will find it more difficult to reel right off exactly what they're after.

In either case, it is important for you to clarify your desires by putting them in writing.

☆ The Power of Desire

Norman Vincent Peale, in his book *The Power of Positive Thinking*,[1] which is the great inspirational best-seller of our time, writes: "A major key to success in this life, to attaining that which you deeply desire, is to be completely released and throw all there is of yourself into your job or any project in which you are engaged. In other words, whatever you are doing, give it all you've got. Give every bit of yourself. Hold nothing back. Life cannot deny itself to the person who gives life his all. But most people, unfortunately, don't do that. In fact, very few people do, and this is a tragic cause of failure, or, if not failure, it is the reason we only half attain."

One of the main reasons why most people never really put their hearts into anything is that they never take the time to define exactly what it is that their hearts desire. But this is so easily remedied by anyone who WILL take the time! And once you know what your heart desires, things begin to happen to you IMME-DIATELY.

As Emerson said, "Beware of what you want for you will get it."

It's truly remarkable what a person can accomplish once he sets his mind to it. As we have said, human desire is the greatest motivating force in human life, and the extent to which a person's desires have been defined and developed determines the extent to which he is motivated to do anything.

In simple terms, it can truly be said that there are only two reasons why anybody desires to do anything:

---

[1] Norman Vincent Peale, *The Power of Positive Thinking*, New York: Prentice-Hall, Inc., 1952.

➡1 Because he desires to *gain* something.

➡2 Because he desires to *avoid losing* something.

What a person desires to gain and what he desires to avoid losing depends on his whole PHILOSOPHY OF LIFE. What a person's standards of living are, what his standards of taste and values are, what interests him most, what he believes is important, whether he thinks his life is important, whether he has any conscious reason for existence, all have a fundamental effect on his innermost desires.

Some people gladly arise in the morning because they have something they actually desire to do. But most people struggle out of bed and go through their daily routine just because they are in the habit of doing so, and are afraid of what might happen if they didn't.

Too many lives have no real meaning because people do not know what they want in life. They are too busy to get acquainted with themselves. They never take the time to study their purposes or to explore new horizons.

We are all guilty of brushing off good ideas because we do not take the time to think about them. When a good idea knocks at the door of our mind, we're about as hospitable as a housewife is to a door-to-door salesman. The idea never really has a chance to get in. Usually it's rejected right at the door as being "impractical" or "something to think about later on."

So the first thing you've got to learn is how to be more receptive to your inner desires no matter how unachievable or how fantastic they may seem to be when you first think of them.

The best way for you to find out how to put your own desires down on paper is to study how others have done this. So I am going to give you a number of actual cases—covering a number of men and women of various ages, who have faced a wide variety of situations and who have succeeded in getting their desires on paper.

As you will see, these cases are not unique or exceptional. In fact, I have deliberately selected cases that are typical and representative—cases of people who have faced common everyday problems with which you are familiar.

As you read these cases, you will begin to think of your own desires in relation to money, love, ego food, and health. *Make a note of every idea you get* as you go along.

✿ Drifting Leads to Resignation

Too many people just *drift* into a job or a marriage, without much forethought; and then when things don't turn out too well they are inclined to resign themselves to an uncomfortable or unpleasant situation, instead of listening to their inner desires and using their imaginations and ingenuity to fulfill these desires.

And this is exactly the situation in which Harry McM. found himself when he came to me for help about three years ago.

Harry, a young salesman, aged twenty-eight, had been married to Rose G. for two years. He was working for his father, selling women's dresses in the New York area, and he didn't like it. He wanted to change to a more interesting field, but he didn't know how.

I asked Harry one of my favorite questions: "Suppose you were financially independent and perfectly free to do anything you wanted, what life work would you select?"

"Well, if I had a free choice," Harry told me, "I'd

teach marketing to college students. I taught Sunday School when I was in my 'teens and I did some teaching while I was in the Army, and I love it. In fact, I like everything about the atmosphere of a college campus, and I certainly don't like the highly competitive atmosphere of the women's dress business and all the high-powered price-cutting eager beavers I have to deal with in this business. But I'm *not* financially independent and making a living in a teaching job is something else again."

"What are your financial requirements?" I asked him.

"Right now I'm making around $10,000 a year. But I've got a chance to make $20,000 or even $25,000 a year within a few years if everything goes all right. You can't make that kind of money teaching school."

And this brings up one of the main reasons why so many people do not follow their desires. Without thinking things through at all, or exploring possibilities further, they simply reject a good idea for "financial reasons." "What makes you think you can't make $20,000 a year in educational work?" I asked Harry.

"Well, I'm a college graduate, and I know that a lot of my college teachers made only $12,000 or $14,000 a year."

"Yes," I agreed. "But I also know a number of men who teach marketing in college. And some of them add to their teaching salaries by acting as marketing consultants to large companies and they enjoy incomes of well over $50,000 a year."

This was news to Harry. But he could easily have found this out himself if he had only taken the time to pursue his original desire a little further instead of rejecting it at the very outset for "financial reasons."

"But don't a lot of these men you're talking about have their Ph.D.'s?" was Harry's next question.

"Yes, they do. And I see no reason why you can't get a Ph.D., too."

At this point, Harry seemed thoroughly amused. The idea seemed too fantastic to be given any serious consideration.

"There are only two questions," he smiled. "What do I use for money while I'm getting it? And what would my wife say to all this?"

"In spite of all the problems involved, Harry, just put your desires down on paper—in relation to money, love, ego food, and health. We'll take up the problems later on, one by one, as they come up."

A week later I saw Harry again, and he handed me a sheet of paper on which he had defined his desires as follows:

1. *MONEY.* I want to make $10,000 this year, and I want to be making $20,000 or over five years from now.

2. *LOVE.* I know that if I went out on my own instead of depending on my father for my job, Rose would think a lot more of me.

3. *EGO FOOD.* Obviously I would enjoy more prestige as a college professor, and I'd think more of myself if I did what I wanted to do.

4. *HEALTH.* Selling women's dresses is beginning to get me down. I've got butterflies in my stomach half the time. Half the people in the business have ulcers. Give me a couple more years at it and I'll have them too. I know I'd feel better if I were doing something I enjoyed more.

We'll come back to Harry in the following chapter.

Florence Q., aged twenty-six and single, came to me with quite another problem.

She wanted to get married. And all her other desires seemed to revolve about that.

Florence had gone to secretarial school when she graduated from high school. And when I first talked to her, she had a job as secretary in a cosmetic plant in the

New York area and was living with her folks on Long Island.

Florence was attractive enough, but she was the reserved type and didn't date much in high school. She didn't meet any eligible men at secretarial school because naturally her classes were made up exclusively of females. And when she got to her job at the cosmetic plant, all the younger men she met there were either married or already spoken for.

Another thing, Florence didn't seem to think that "living at home" was helping her much on this score. But she hesitated to come right out and tell her parents that she would like to get a New York apartment with a couple of other girls. Besides, she wasn't making enough money to support that kind of luxury.

Obviously, the first thing Florence had to do to make her beginning move—which would be to get a place in New York City so she could spend more time with people her own age and get more active socially—was to make more money. And it is equally obvious that in order to make more money, it was necessary for Florence to get into some kind of job that paid more money.

"Tell me, Florence," I asked, "what really interests you most? What kind of job would you get a real kick out of?"

"I've often thought I'd like personnel work," she told me. "Every time I go into the personnel office in the company, I find myself envying the people who interview young women applying for work. On the other hand, what I'm doing is beginning to bore me stiff. I don't see enough people on a job like this."

"Then why don't you get into personnel work?" I asked.

"Why . . . they don't pay secretaries in the personnel department any more than they pay in the production department where I am. And that's all I know how to do. I've never had any training in personnel."

"No, you don't have any training now. But I see no reason why you can't get it."

"But I don't even have a college education, and I don't see how in the world I can go to school and qualify for a job in personnel administration when I've got to work for a living and I'm hardly earning enough now to make both ends meet."

"I didn't say you have to be a college graduate to get into personnel work," I assured her. "Just go ahead and put your desires down on paper in relation to money, love, ego food, and health, and don't worry at this stage about HOW you're going to get the things you want."

Within a few weeks she came to me with the following definitions:

1. *MONEY.* I'd really have to be making about $250 a week before I could feel financially independent enough to live in New York. That's what Grace and Joan make: they've got an apartment in New York and they don't save much money either. But they've both got good jobs.

2. *LOVE.* Naturally I want to get married and raise a family. But I don't want to take the first guy who comes along. And I'm certainly not going to meet anyone interesting out around home, because I know the young people there and practically all my friends are married. I want to meet some attractive and intelligent young men who have the same ideas about living as I do.

3. *EGO FOOD.* I'm certainly not getting any challenge on my present job, and I know I could get more excited about personnel work, especially if I could land a responsible job I'd be real proud of.

4. *HEALTH.* Health is the one thing I've got. That is, physical health. And I want to keep it. But I know I'd feel better mentally if I were doing something more interesting, and if I had more dates.

We'll meet Florence again in a later chapter.

✿ Middle-age Problems

However, you may be a little further along in life than Harry McM. or Florence Q., and, as you know, middle-aged people have different problems.

For example, the middle-aged man with heavy family responsibilities who has spent considerable time in one line of work and has been reasonably successful at it, usually balks at the idea of changing jobs. Even though he isn't particularly happy and even though there is something else he would rather do, he is inclined to feel that he's got to play it safe. He hesitates to consider any kind of new field because of the financial risks.

That was Thomas D.'s situation when he called on me.

Thomas D., forty-three years old, was controller of a canned food company in New England. At our first meeting, he squirmed in his chair, talked of vague aches and pains. He was working day and night and was not only approaching a nervous collapse from overwork but his wife was threatening to leave him.

Our conversation revealed that in the canned food business, he was spending practically all his time in an office dealing with "things," whereas his yearnings were to deal more with people. He had participated in several fund-raising campaigns for local hospitals and he showed an unusually sympathetic interest in hospitals and all the financial problems they have to meet in order to keep their facilities in step with the great advances in medicine—especially in serving needy persons who are unable to pay for the latest and best kind of treatment.

"If I were as vitally interested in hospitals as you seem to be," I told him, "I'd get into hospital work."

"Yes, but the canned food business is the only business I know," was his quick comeback. "Here I am in my forties with a wife and three children. What chance have I got to make a switch at this late date?"

"We shall see what chance you've got," I said. "But first of all I want you to explore thoroughly your interest in hospitals by putting down on paper your inner desires in relation to money, love, ego food, and health."

Here's the statement Thomas D. came up with:

1. *MONEY.* I've been making $17,000 a year at my present job and I need that much to live on. But I want to get up to at least $20,000 within the next few years. The children are growing up and it won't be long until they need some help to go to college. And I can make $20,000 if I stay in the canned food business.

2. *LOVE.* I've got to spend more time with my wife and family and rebuild our relationship before it's too late—if it's not too late now. On my present job, I've got to go to an out-of-town plant for a day or two almost every week, and my wife doesn't like it. Even when I'm in town, I neglect my family because I carry too much stuff home with me to work on at night.

3. *EGO FOOD.* I don't mind the canned food business. It's an important business. But I'd feel a lot more important if I could do an outstanding job in some humanitarian field. I like people and I'd like to feel that I was helping people who really need me.

4. *HEALTH.* I've been overworking and I know it. I've been grumpy around the house. Haven't felt too well for several years now. I realize I've got to adopt more sensible work habits. My family doctor has told me I've got to slow up. And I think if I were in a "people" business, this would definitely improve my mental outlook.

This case, like the others, will be picked up later.

☼ Housewives Can Get Their Hearts' Desires

Now, if you're a housewife, you may still feel that it's futile to daydream. As I have already observed, housewives, especially those who are pretty well occupied with the job of raising a family, usually fall into the class of those "whose work is never done," and it isn't easy for a woman so occupied to extricate herself from the "daily chores" and to pursue her heart's desire.

Mary T. and Helen A. were both in the same boat.

They both had two children—one in grade school and one in high school. They both had their hands full raising their children and running a home. They both wanted some active outside interest to take their minds off housework, and had often commiserated about it.

But suddenly the similarity ended.

Mary T.'s husband had a sudden operation and died. He left some insurance, but just enough to pay off the mortgage on their home with a little left over. So Mary T. was suddenly faced with the problem of getting a job and earning enough money to keep her family together until the children were grown up and able to take care of themselves.

Faced with that kind of pressure, Mary T. got on her horse and did something about it—quick.

Helen A. took more time to do anything about her problem.

Certainly I don't like to see anyone fall victim to any kind of trouble. But let's face it. We are all inclined to be as lazy as we dare to be, and it's always a thrilling thing to observe a human being respond to a sudden challenge.

One of the main things wrong with most people is that they go along day by day following an easy existence and taking the most important blessings of life—their own health and the health and love of their family—for granted. They may talk about doing this or that in order to improve themselves or to make life more interesting. But they keep putting off doing anything about it, because they are never inspired and they are never forced into action by some sudden misfortune. Consequently, they live and die without reaching anywhere near their full possibilities for development and achievement.

As Mary T. said, just after she lost her husband, "I didn't know when I was lucky. Now every single day when I first wake up, I thank God that the children and I have our health and that we are all bound together with a strong bond of mutual understanding, respect, and love for each other.

"Another thing—I used to think I was pretty busy. And I was. But now that I've begun to explore job possibilities, I can see that I used to spend an awful lot of time fussing around with little things that aren't important at all. If anyone had told me, a year ago, that I could spend three or four hours a day on outside interests and still run a home, I'd have told him he was crazy. But that's exactly what I've been doing for the past month or so, and as soon as I make up my mind what kind of job I'm after, I expect to spend still more time making a living. And I'll run my home the way it ought to be run, too, because I've *got* to do it."

Yes, Mary T. knew within three months after her husband died exactly what she wanted in relation to:

1. *MONEY*. With our home paid for, we can live on about $10,000 a year.

2. *LOVE*. All I want now is the love and respect of my children.

3. *EGO FOOD*. I'd be proud to teach English in high school and my children would be proud cf me, too. And I would feel that I was making a contribution to my community.

4. *HEALTH*. Fortunately, I've got my health and now I've got to do everything I can to keep it.

While there were financial problems to be solved while she prepared to teach school and actually land a job, Mary T. simply looked upon these problems as problems that could and would be solved.

After all, problems don't "buffalo" you so much when you're "running scared."

On the other hand, it took Helen A. over a year to decide:

1. *MONEY.* Since money is not a problem with me, I'd be satisfied if I could just make a little "extra" money at some outside interest.

2. *LOVE.* I already have the love of my husband and my children and the important thing is to continue to cultivate that love, and to choose some outside interest that won't interfere with the time I should spend on my family.

3. *EGO FOOD.* I like to paint landscapes, and if I took some lessons and spent at least two hours a day at it, I feel that I might turn out some good stuff and maybe sell a few paintings.

4. *HEALTH.* The only thing I can think of on this score is that I might feel better if I ate a little less and lost about 15 pounds.

We'll return to Mary T. and Helen A. later.

☆ Prepare for the Years to Come

Incidentally, as a career counselor I have had a great deal of trouble trying to persuade middle-aged people that they are going to grow older, and that they SHOULD, during the middle years, prepare themselves avocationally for some compelling reason for existence later in life; and that if they don't, they will certainly deteriorate mentally and physically long before their time.

Most middle-aged people just don't seem to believe this, or they would act differently.

Just last winter, Harvey H., whom I had counseled some ten years ago, was back on my doorstep. I took one look at the tight grim expression around his lips, and I could see that he was seriously concerned about something.

"Looks like this is it," he said hopelessly. "Looks like

the end of the line for me. I guess they mean it when they say that sixty-five is the compulsory retirement age with our company. I'll be sixty-five in March and they are already planning a farewell testimonial dinner for me. It's all kind of crazy, if you ask me. I'm not old. I'm still a good production engineer. I know my job. And I can do a good job. But I'm out—come next March. And where am I going to land the kind of job I've been used to? Who's going to hire a man sixty-five years old?"

This is not an unusual experience for me. In fact, I find an alarming increase in problem cases among older men who suddenly lose their jobs and find considerable difficulty trying to get relocated.

There is no real excuse for this unhappy situation.

After all, life is predictable.

We all know that, because of the blessings of medical science and the great advances that have been made in the improvement of our diet, we have a much better chance of living far beyond sixty-five than our ancestors had.

And yet most men fail, in their prime, to look forward to the later years and to make adequate preparation so they can anticipate these years with pleasure instead of dread.

☼ Start Your Own Business

Even though a man fails to make adequate preparation for the later years, and doesn't even think about the problem until he's suddenly forced to, this doesn't mean that it's too late to do anything about it or that he should give up all hope.

And I told Harvey H. so.

I told Harvey about a retired office manager who got tired of being sore at the world in general and who decided to start a small printing business of his own. Beginning with nothing but a mimeographing machine, he soon acquired a hand press and is now doing a nice business on small printing jobs that he gets right in his own neighborhood.

I told Harvey about a retired sales manager who went into the travel service business and is living in Florida. He loves to fish and he has always wanted an excuse to live in Florida. Now he has developed a profitable business there. He arranges vacation trips for the tired executives he used to work with in New York. He handles their transportation, hotel reservations, fishing boat rentals, and takes care of anything else they want.

I told Harvey about the retired newspaper editor who now owns a small weekly newspaper, the retired carpenter who now runs a hunting lodge in Canada, the retired merchandising manager who now acts as a business consultant specializing in retail store advertising devices for large national advertisers, the retired salesman who now operates a water softener business, the retired mechanic who operates a radio repair service in an old garage, and the retired advertising agency copywriter who now operates a small direct-mail advertising agency.

Then I suggested to Harvey that he put his own desires down on paper, and a month or so later he came back, enthusiastic, with the following statement:

1. *MONEY.* Although my children are raised and there's no one except my wife and me, and we own our own home, I still need $10,000 or $12,000 a year if I'm to continue to live the way I've been living.

2. *LOVE.* I've got no real problem here, but I know my wife and my children would think a lot more of me if I continued to work and to grow in the engineering profession.

3. *EGO FOOD.* I'm well known in this part of New York State, and I got quite a kick out of visiting some of the plants in this area and talking about some of their problems. There's quite

a shortage of engineers, and I have found out that I can make a pretty good living acting as trouble shooter and engineering consultant. Another thing, avocationally, I'd like to do some writing for some of the professional magazines which I've never had the time to do up till now. After all, there's no ego food like seeing your name in print.

4. *HEALTH*. I've been complaining about a few aches and pains, but my doctor says it's only old age creeping in. I'm convinced now that if I didn't have time to think about them, they wouldn't bother me so much. In fact, just anticipating the possibility of having nothing to do when I retire in March made me feel terrible. I'm beginning to feel better already, now that I'm satisfied that I can go into business for myself.

Harvey H. was pretty well off in comparison with many people who face this same problem.

Joe C. and his life had to sell their home in Pittsburgh in order to get enough money to buy a small combination house and hardware store on the Jersey coast where they are now happily making a living running the hardware store and renting rooms to summer residents.

And Jim M. and his wife had to sell their home in Chicago to get enough money to buy a small ranch house and some acreage in Arizona where they are now getting along very well raising and selling livestock.

✿ Older Women Have Their Opportunities Too

Older women have their problems, too.

Elsie van M. was in her late fifties. Her family was raised. Her husband traveled a lot. And she was lonely.

When she got up in the morning, wondering what to do with herself, she often—too often—wound up visiting her married daughter who lived nearby. Then she often —too often—stayed for dinner. Her son-in-law got fed up with having her around so much. One evening he blew up and told her so.

That was enough to start Elsie thinking.

In her younger days, she had been a top secretary in one of the biggest companies in town.

To improve her standing with her children, to become a more interesting person to her husband, to get some much needed ego food, to make some money of her own, and to gain a greater feeling of financial security for the rest of her life, Elsie suddenly decided to go in for secretarial work again. And later on, we'll see exactly how she went about it.

If you are a woman in the middle years, whose family is raised—or even if you've never had a family—put your desires down on paper and get ready to do something about achieving your desires.

There are plenty of women who have solved this problem.

I know a widow in St. Louis who, threatened with the prospect of financial hardship in her fifties, decided that she could sell younger men and women on the wisdom of insuring themselves against such risks. It was weeks before she sold her first policy. But before the first year had gone by, she had sold more annuity contracts than any other salesman in her company.

Agnes U. was a baby sitter, living in northern New Jersey, when she decided to take a few courses of study and to qualify herself to run a small nursery school in her home for which there seemed to be a real demand in her community. She's doing very well at this.

The woman who tutors high school students in French and Latin, the woman who runs a telephone answering service, the woman who does bedside teaching to children who are ill, the woman who clerks part time in the local drugstore—these are among thousands of women who are thoroughly enjoying the later years.

☆ *Take Things One Step at a Time*

The moment you begin to contemplate doing something new, you are inclined to be discouraged at the very outset when you begin thinking of all the difficulties involved in the second and the third and the fourth and the following steps in your program. So *don't permit your mind to become swamped with a maze of problems that cannot be solved all at once.* When you undertake *one step at a time*, you'll find that a satisfactory solution to each step is relatively easy to arrive at. And as you progress through this book, you'll learn how to take each step in the proper order.

"But wait a minute," you might say. "I can think of a number of things that I'd like to do, but that doesn't mean that I can just up and do them."

And my answer to you is this:

You CERTAINLY CAN UP AND DO anything that you really WANT TO DO, providing it makes sense and providing you undertake to do it *one step at a time*. And DON'T YOU EVER FORGET IT!

The important thing is that you don't up and kick a good idea out the window before you give it or yourself a chance. THERE IS FAR TOO MUCH NEGATIVE THINKING IN THIS WORLD. THERE IS FAR TOO MUCH RESIGNING ONESELF TO AN UNCOMFORTABLE OR UNSATISFACTORY SITUATION.

The main thing, at this stage, is not to reject ANY IDEA of what you might like to do. Just let yourself go. Dream a little. No matter how impractical an idea may seem, and no matter how many reasons you can think of why you could never do such a thing, go ahead and make a note of it. Put it down in writing. We'll test it out in the following chapter and find out whether it makes sense or not—in light of your abilities, your capacity in human relations, and in light of ALL the things you want out of life.

☆ How To Get Things Down on Paper

Now, I KNOW you are ready to begin to put YOUR personal desires down on paper—in relation to MONEY, LOVE, EGO FOOD, and HEALTH.

MONEY—You will have no difficulty if you begin by making a note of the *amount of money you want to make for the coming year* and then just add a rough estimate of what you would like to be making *five years from now*.

LOVE—You're married or you're not. If you're married, the main question is *whether you're working at it or not*. If you're not doing everything you can to make a success of your marriage, *write down what you ought to be doing*.

If you're not married, you probably want to get married. And you either have a good prospect in mind or you don't. If you have a good prospect in mind, put down on paper what YOU ought to be doing to bring the marriage about. If you don't have a good prospect, put down on paper what YOU ought to be doing in order to MEET some good prospects.

EGO FOOD—You know, by now, that *men and career women* who like their jobs and who are genuinely interested in and proud of what they're doing, *get ego food from their work*; that *housewives get ego food from raising a family and making a good home*; and that all three can get *additional ego food* they may desire by working at part-time jobs, pursuing favorite hobbies, and taking an active interest in various community activities.

Write down exactly where you stand on ego food. And if you're *not getting enough* of it, *write down all the possibilities* you can think of for getting it.

HEALTH—If you're sick, you're probably already doing something about it. If you enjoy good health and have no bad health habits, congratulations! But if you're like most people, you could do with a few health reminders to yourself.

So if you smoke, drink, work, eat, weigh, or run around too much, make a note of it and write down what you're going to do to correct the situation.

Briefly, then, if you follow the procedure given in this chapter, you will have no difficulty in defining your personal desires and putting them down on paper.

And then you will suddenly find that THINGS BEGIN TO HAPPEN TO YOU.

For, as Lincoln said, "Your own resolution to succeed is more important than any other one thing."

THIS CHAPTER—IN A NUTSHELL

✔ 1. DESIRE IS THE GREATEST MOTIVATING FORCE IN HUMAN LIFE.

✔ 2. BE RECEPTIVE to your INNER DESIRES and put them down on paper—no matter how unachievable they may seem when you first think of them.

✔ 3. WRITE DOWN IN YOUR NOTEBOOK under MONEY, LOVE, EGO FOOD, and HEALTH, exactly WHAT YOUR DESIRES ARE.

6

DO YOUR

ABILITIES AND

HUMAN RELATIONS

SUPPORT YOUR

DESIRES?

As a rule, a person's natural abilities point in the same direction as his desires, and when a person is doing what he *likes to do* and what he *can do well,* he is a lot *easier to get along with* than when he is performing some distasteful task at which he is inept.

It is also true that ordinarily a person just naturally gravitates toward the kind of people he enjoys most and can get along with best.

Therefore, it is not surprising that our most realistic and achievable desires are so often suggested by the things we *can do best* and when we are with the *people we enjoy most.*

Remember Harry McM., the young salesman who didn't like the dress business and who wanted to get into the college teaching field. His *desire* came from his *natural ability to teach,* which he discovered in the Army, and from his strong preference for the *human relations environment of the college campus* over the highly competitive commercial environment of the women's dress business.

As is usually the case, it was necessary for Harry to get some additional training before he could hope to land the job he was after and to make the money he desired. But, because his natural ability and preference in human relations supported his desires, he could be reasonably sure that his desires were achievable.

Now getting down to your own case, let's see how you can proceed to find out whether YOUR abilities and YOUR human relations support YOUR desires.

✡ *Do Your Abilities Support Your Desires?*

No matter what vocational, part-time, or other activity you are considering, if you have had some practical experience that has revealed that you have the natural ability to do what you want to do, you are on pretty sure ground.

If you have *not* had such practical experience, there is no difficulty in finding out what abilities are required in any field you are considering. All you have to do is talk with a few leaders and workers in that field. You'll soon find out whether you've got what it takes and whether you can acquire the necessary abilities in a reasonable length of time.

Naturally, if you think you want to be a great opera singer and you haven't got the "pipes," or if you think you want to be a dentist or a surgeon and you haven't got the "hands," or if you think you want to be a great engineer or a scientist and you haven't got the "brain," you'd better forget it. However, the most important thing is: DO NOT CONFUSE BASIC ABILITY WITH *TRAINING*.

Lawrence Tibbett failed to make the high school glee club. But that didn't mean that he did not have the *ability* to become a great singer. It simply meant that his voice at that time was untrained and undeveloped.

Albert Einstein, author of the Theory of Relativity and certainly one of the greatest mathematicians who ever lived, failed in the entrance examinations of the Federal Polytechnic College of Zurich when he was sixteen years of age. But this did not mean that Einstein lacked the *ability* to become a great scientist. It simply meant that he had to do some more cramming before he took his second examination and was admitted.

☆ Don't Misinterpret Your Experience

Another thing to look out for is misinterpreting your experience. One young man who was weak in mathematics in high school told me that he would like to study engineering but didn't think that he'd be able to make the grade because of his high-school record. However, after a two-year tour in the Army Signal Corps, he became so interested in electronics that he was determined to be an engineer. He took some night-school courses in mathematics to prove he could make good grades. And now he's doing very well in one of the top engineering schools in the country.

Time after time I have seen "strength" spring from "weakness" when a "strong desire" was present. Remember Miss Tenley Albright from Boston. When she was just seventeen years old, she became the first United States girl ever to win the World's Figure Skating Championship, thereby capping a courageous six-year comeback from polio.

Then, too, you yourself must know people who have

been "scared off" certain fields because they did not succeed in, or maybe were even fired from, a certain job. Under the proper supervision and leadership, they might do very well in such a job—if they REALLY WANTED TO.

✪ What Is Your Main Function?

Here's another thought that will help you immeasurably in finding out where you fit best, ability-wise, in any job or outside activity you are considering.

In every business, art, trade, or profession, there are four major functions to be performed:

▶▶1. *Creative work*—inventing, discovering, or developing new ideas.

▶▶2. *Administrative work*—making plans and policies for the conduct and supervision of the entire business or project.

▶▶3. *Executive work*—directing the work of others in actually carrying out plans and policies in one or more departments.

▶▶4. *Line work*—performing 'some individual task involving no responsibility for the work of others.

✪ Do You Have Creative Ability?

If you have creative ability, you probably know it without anybody telling you. Your creative talents have demanded expression in your early youth. If there is any doubt in your mind as to whether you have the ability to invent or to discover or to develop new ideas, you probably do not have this ability. And even if you think you have it, if you have never built or made or designed or invented or written or painted or created anything original that particularly pleased you and that you considered to be your very own, you probably do not have creative ability. If you do have any kind of creative ability, it might be one of your best cues as to what you'd like to do.

✿ Do You Have Administrative Ability?

If you are a thoughtful person, slow to act, who enjoys analyzing, interpreting, and patiently summarizing the results of the activities of others; if you're the kind of person who likes to pry into every single phase of an operation and to view a business or activity as a whole; if you get a big kick out of cautiously defining long-range plans and policies; if you're strong on logic, figures, and finance, you have the most important earmarks of an able administrator.

✿ Do You Have Executive Ability?

If you like people, if you like action, if you like to organize and direct other people as they carry out plans and policies that are handed to you by an over-all administrator; if you enjoy the responsibility of seeing to it that these people who work for you do the job well and get it done on time; and if you're perfectly content to confine your activities to the one department of the business or activity you are responsible for, you'll probably make a first-rate executive.

✿ Are You a Line Worker?

Of course, you know as well as I do, that there are many people who do not have creative ability or administrative ability and who have no desire to assume executive responsibility for the work of others. And after all, there are a lot of individual tasks that are satisfying and even fascinating. As one salesman told me, "I get a big kick out of my job, selling. How much I make depends entirely on my own efforts. I don't want to be a supervisor. I don't want to have to worry at night about what some other salesman did or did not do."

While it is true that a person can possess more than one of these four kinds of abilities, in most instances he is best able to perform either a creative or an administrative or an executive or a line function. Many an able salesman has ruined himself trying to be a sales manager; many an able mechanic has failed trying to be a foreman; and many an able executive or creative person has gotten ulcers trying to be a business administrator.

☼ What Is Your Tempo?

Another important point to check in considering your ability to do any job is whether you enjoy working at a fast tempo under pressure or prefer to work at a relatively slow pace. A lot of people with a slow tempo crack up when they work in a fast-moving environment, and a lot of people with a fast tempo get plain bored if they work at a job where things move too slowly.

When Eddie G., a young newspaperman, came to me for help he was so nervous and upset that he began sobbing soon after he began to talk about his job. His writing abilities were well developed and that's the reason he went into newspaper work in the first place.

But the fast pace of the newsroom was too much for him. While it was true that he could write, he did his best writing when he had plenty of time to think everything out and write thoughtfully.

After a thorough study of his case, Eddie and I decided he should take a job teaching in a New England boys' preparatory school and write the things he really wanted to write in his leisure hours. In three years, on his teaching job, he turned out two books—one in the field of music appreciation and one in the field of economics. The last time I had lunch with him, he was beaming. I have never seen a happier person. He told me that he felt whole and adequate for the first time in his life.

☼ Do Your Human Relations Support Your Desires?

No matter what your desires may be, if you have had some practical experience that has shown you have the capacity for getting along with the people who are involved in their realization, then your desires pass the human relations test.

If you have *not* had such practical experience, you had better check your desire by meeting some of these people for the purpose of finding out, in advance, how much you think you would enjoy working with them.

However, I will say this. Ordinarily, it is relatively easy to acquire the necessary capacity to get along with the people you may find in any job or outside activity— if you are REALLY ENTHUSIASTIC about it. In fact, I have seen people turn into masters in human relations almost overnight as soon as it dawned on them that unless they improved their attitudes toward people, they could never hope to achieve their desired objectives.

However, if you are not naturally aggressive and competitive, you probably would be unhappy as a house-to-house salesman. And if you can't take a lot of unjustified criticism in public, you had better not run for public office.

Certainly success or failure in anything you undertake can turn on your capacity in human relations.

Harry W. is not strong in human relations, and he doesn't have to be on his particular job. He is happy testing and working out new ideas and improvements for navigational instruments that are used in industry because he's mechanically inclined and he likes to work alone.

On the other hand, Tommy T. is highly competitive in his human relations and enjoys meeting new people. He likes being with men and women who are interested in marketing and sales. Consequently, when he came to me for help he was in a bad way mentally because he was working in the production department of an advertising agency. He felt inadequate and out of place. He was, for that job. He was a good technician in making advertising layouts and selecting type faces, but practically all his work was done alone. When we added up his desires and talents, it seemed obvious that he might make a crackerjack salesman for some technical line. I encouraged him to apply for a sales job with a leading publisher of trade magazines. He got the job, is making much more money than he ever made before, and he's well cast for the first time in his life. "I'm really living now," he told me.

And Gladys J., who enjoys meeting new people and talking with them about anything and everything, gets a big kick out of her part-time job, and likes the extra money she makes, as a house-to-house interviewer on readership research for a leading women's magazine.

Don F., who likes people all right but who prefers to have them come to him, is an outstanding success managing a supermarket, while Mary V., who has two small children and who still loves babies, thoroughly enjoys spending three hours on two evenings a week as a volunteer worker in the maternity ward of a nearby hospital.

Some jobs and part-time activities require that you

actively and aggressively persuade others to your point of view: Cedric W. is made to order for his job selling insurance, while Florence R. is one of the top part-time house-to-house saleswomen with a leading cosmetic manufacturer.

Arthur B. prefers the educational atmosphere of a college campus and is a highly successful teacher and business researcher in a southwestern university; while Nancy D., who has the same tastes, is a secretary and statistical worker in the psychology department at the same university.

And Audrey M., who prefers the educational environment of the secondary school, teaches in a nearby private school. She has a teen-age son who attends the same school.

So whether you like to work alone or rub shoulders with other people, whether you like to take the initiative in meeting people or prefer to have people come to you, whether you like an educational or professional or artistic atmospere or a rough-and-tumble highly competitive trade or business, your tastes in human relations have a lot to do with your selection of what you want to do. For if you do not enjoy the human relations involved in any job or outside activity, sooner or later you're bound to get fed up with it.

However, even after you are satisfied that your abilities and human relations support your desires, does this mean that you will go ahead and do anything about it?

Not necessarily.

Unfortunately, there are three common excuses which many people give for not doing what they say they would like to do.

In the next chapter we shall see how you can free your mind from these negative and destructive mental attitudes.

POINTS TO REMEMBER

✔ 1. Our soundest desires come from what we can DO BEST and the human relations we ENJOY MOST.

✔ 2. DOUBLE-CHECK YOUR ABILITIES AND YOUR HUMAN RELATIONS to be sure your desires are REALISTIC AND ACHIEVABLE.

✔ 3. DON'T CONFUSE ABILITY WITH TRAINING.

✔ 4. STRENGTH OFTEN SPRINGS FROM WEAKNESS when a STRONG DESIRE is present.

✔ 5. You can IMPROVE YOUR HUMAN RELATIONS OVERNIGHT when you're doing what you WANT to do.

7

THE THREE

COMMON EXCUSES

You MAY KNOW WHAT YOU WANT OUT OF LIFE IN terms of money, love, ego food, and health, and your desires may square with your abilities and your human relations. But this doesn't mean a thing unless you DO SOMETHING about it—unless you begin to move one step at a time toward the realization of your desires.

The whole trouble with most people is that even when they DO KNOW what they want, they keep postponing "doing anything about it." And when you stall and make excuses for postponing action, you are DOOMED TO STAY WHERE YOU ARE.

To put things off is so easy, especially if you kid yourself with the fallacy that you will be better able to go ahead some time in the future than you are right now.

THERE IS NOTHING MAGICAL ABOUT THE FUTURE!

The future, when it comes, is JUST LIKE THE PRESENT.

You can begin to build your future TODAY. The present is all you have. And the opportunity of the present is worth more than any success you have enjoyed in the past or any action you might postpone for the future.

Actually, most of us live in a curious dream world. The young live in the promises of the future. The old live in the unembraced opportunities of the past. A young person says, "As soon as I get the time and get a few dollars ahead, I'm going to . . ." The older person says, "If I were young again, I'd . . ."

I have had young people tell me in a loud voice what they DEFINITELY plan to do. I have had older people tell me in a whisper what they always DREAMED OF DOING, but NEVER DID.

For over twenty years now, in confidential sessions with men and women—young, middle-aged, and older—I've been asking people why they do NOT do what they SAY they want to do, and I haven't heard a new excuse for years.

It's always one or more of three common excuses:

> ▸▸"I haven't the time."
> ▸▸"I haven't the money."
> ▸▸"My folks wouldn't approve."

✿ Fighting Ghosts

For instance, remember Harry McM., the dress salesman who wanted to become a college professor. To begin with, he had two excuses for not pursuing this desire: money and folks. He couldn't see how he could make enough money as a college teacher, and he didn't think his wife would approve of anything that would drastically reduce his pay check.

Now Harry knows that he was "fighting ghosts." Now he knows that he can satisfy his financial desires as a college teacher *and* as a business consultant. And now that he has talked the whole thing over with his wife, he knows that his wife not only approves of his program, but she has more respect and admiration for him than she ever had before and is eager to do everything she can to help him with his program. In fact, she told me personally that she is so proud of Harry that she can hardly keep still about him.

Remember Florence Q., the secretary to the production manager in a cosmetic factory, who wanted to study personnel administration and move to New York. But she couldn't see where she would ever get the *money* to take courses and to live in New York, and she hesitated to discuss the move with *her family*.

However, when she took the trouble to talk the matter over with her employer, she found out that her company had a long-standing policy of paying tuition for night-school courses taken by employees who wished to improve their positions in the company. And when she discussed the matter with her parents, they finally had to agree that her plan was a good one for her. So Florence found out that she had been "fighting ghosts," too.

Remember Thomas D., the forty-three-year old controller of a canned food company who wanted to move into the hospital field and who didn't think he could "make the switch" for "money" reasons. Well, he found out, in a series of discussions with the authorities in several hospitals where he had served as a fund-raiser, that he could make as much money acting as business manager of a New England hospital as he could make if he continued as controller for the canned goods company.

And remember Mary T. and Helen A., busy housewives who never felt that they "had the time" to pursue any outside interest—seriously. But when Mary T. lost her husband and was suddenly faced with the problem of getting a job, she immediately began to make more efficient use of her time—because she *had to*. And Helen A., inspired by Mary's courageous example, ultimately found that she too could find the time seriously to pursue her interest in painting.

In the next chapter, we'll see how all these people proceeded to solve their problems, one step at a time.

I could recite hundreds of cases to you—all showing that the common excuses we have for not doing what we want to do are merely "ghosts" that disappear in thin air when we get on our horse and get into action.

Nevertheless, no matter what desires *you* have put down on paper, you are probably bothered, right now, by one or more of these three common excuses that keep you from going ahead and taking your first step NOW.

So let's take a good square look at these three common excuses so that you can see, once and for all time, that they really don't hold water, so that you can free your mind of these negative and destructive mental attitudes, and so that you can proceed with YOUR first step toward the realization of your inner desires.

✿ What About TIME?

It is generally recognized and accepted that only the busiest people ever have time for anything.

The next time that you "haven't the time" to do what you REALLY want to do, it may be worth while for you to remember that you have as much time as anyone else

—twenty-four hours a day. And how you spend much of that time is really up to you.

Whatever your present situation may be, if you will put down in your notebook how you have spent each hour of the day for the past seven days, and then keep a record of how you spend each hour for the next seven days, I think you'll change your mind about not having the time. You may not have ALL the time you'd LIKE for what you want to do, but you do have enough time TO GET STARTED.

When I examined the daily schedule of Peter H., a paper salesman who told me he wanted to get into advertising but didn't have the time to take a course of study that was being offered by the local advertising club, I found that he had gone to the movies two evenings and attended a dance one evening of the previous week.

And when I examined the daily schedule of a "busy" housewife who told me she wanted to write short stories but hadn't the time, right then, to take a correspondence course and get down to serious writing, I found that she had played bridge two afternoons and watched television for several hours on five evenings of the previous week.

I'm not suggesting for a moment that you give up all your diversions. But I think you will be surprised to learn the small part of your time you need to devote, in the beginning, to the thing you want to do, and the remarkable achievements possible for anyone who will consistently devote even as little as one hour a day to one single purpose. And the unvarnished truth is that every one of us who mouths the old excuse, "I haven't the time," wastes much more than an hour every day of his life.

So start looking. You'll find a loose hour some place in

your daily schedule. Begin to devote that hour to the thing you want to do most—even if it's merely THINK-ING about what your first step ought to be.

☼ What About MONEY?

As we all know, money comes first in most people's minds and, as a rule, the older we get, the more emphasis we put upon money, the more we think *money*. And so it may be difficult for you to appreciate the fact that money is secondary.

I didn't say money is of no importance. I said it is secondary.

I've seen so many men and women who told me they were "out after the dough" wind up making less money than those who put primary emphasis on what they like to do.

Even if you have a strong desire to accumulate wealth, it's important to remember that the amount of money you earn depends on how valuable and productive you are, and you are certain to become more valuable and more productive if you are doing what you want to do. You'll be a whale of a lot happier, too.

Too many people let their desire for money lure them into a job they dislike or keep them on a job that bores them.

I'm thinking of a young man fresh from high school who had two jobs offered him—one as a mail boy in an advertising agency and one as a machine operator in a cosmetic factory. This young man was very much interested in the advertising business, but he took the factory job because it paid more money.

Now he's unhappy. The factory job bores him. And he'll continue to be unhappy until he realizes that it's a grave mistake for a young man just starting out to select a job on the basis of how much money it pays; that it's far wiser to seek a job in a business he likes, even though it pays less to start with. For if he likes his job, he'll apply himself more earnestly, he'll get more good ideas, and he'll progress faster.

Not long ago, a man in his thirties told me, "I'd like to go into the cattle business, but I haven't got the money."

"You ought to be glad you haven't got the money," I told him.

"What do you mean?" He seemed surprised.

"Well, if you had enough money to go into the cattle business right now, you'd probably lose it. What do you know about the cattle business? If you want to go into this business, the first thing to do is go to work for somebody else and find out something about how the business is run. After you have acquired enough experience and accumulated a little money, then it's time for you to consider going into it on your own."

Now, as far as you, the reader, are concerned, maybe you don't have all the money you'd like to have right now to do what you'd like to do. But you can take the first step toward getting the money you need to begin with.

You may have to hold on to your present job in order to meet your financial requirements while you pursue your favorite interests part-time. But sooner or later, if you keep at it, you will be able to spend most of your time doing what you like best—and meet your financial requirements, too.

I've been career counseling men and women for a good many years now, and the people I have most trouble with are those who *have* money. For once they find out what they really want to do, they are not pressured enough, by economic necessity, to do anything about it.

Neither poverty nor riches has anything to do with the job of self-expression—doing what you want to do—except that the possession of money is likely to remove the pressure of necessity and to lull us into a lazy coma. Financial security, soft living, plenty to eat, an easy chair, comfortable slippers, a warm fire—these are enough to ruin any man.

✡ What About FOLKS?

From the cradle to the grave, we are all in danger of being unduly influenced by the opinions of those who are nearest and dearest to us.

While we are growing up, our parents are likely to dominate, rather than guide, us in the choice of a career. And as soon as we break loose from our mother's apron strings and our father's financial support, we are influenced by what our sweethearts think. Then, when we marry, our husband or wife, as the case may be, may discourage us from following our inner desire.

When Harriet B. told her husband that she would like to run for the local council—and on the OTHER political party ticket!—he strenuously opposed the whole idea. "You'll only make a fool out of yourself!" he told her.

But when she went ahead and ran for office anyway, he suddenly became one of her most ardent supporters, and when she was finally elected to the city council, he was proud as punch!

Wives sometimes have a way of interfering with a man's pursuing his career desires—especially if it involves lower pay or a change in location. But wives can be won over if husbands do not falter.

When Bill M. first told his wife that he had been transferred to Dallas, she raised the dickens because she didn't want to move away from her family and friends in Westchester, and she didn't want to "uproot" the children and have them transferred to another school.

But now that Bill has been made division manager for his company in Dallas, and is making more money than he ever made in New York, his wife can see that the advantages of the move overbalance the disadvantages.

In Part Two of this book, Chapter 10, titled "How To Get Along Better With People," spells out exactly how you can get the understanding and cooperation of your wife or husband or anyone else who should approve your program—if it makes sense and if it's something you really want.

Now I'm not saying that it is impossible for you to get constructive suggestions from "folks" when you talk things over with them. All I'm saying is that it's a big mistake to use "folks" as an excuse for not doing what you want to do. And in the long run, your folks won't thank you for it either.

One thing is certain. You will never venture anything or achieve anything worthwhile if you permit yourself to be unduly influenced by others. It isn't a very pleasant thought, but it is nonetheless true, that some of the worst advice often springs from the short-sighted and selfish interests of those whom we love most.

After all, you will never get the greatest love or the highest respect of those whom you love most by being a colorless, self-conscious, vacillating person who is neither hot nor cold, wet nor dry, because he is always wondering what others will think of him and is always trying to please everybody.

☆ Act As an Individual

But you can earn this love and respect by thinking and acting as an individual. Lose your mental freedom, lose your individuality, and you lose everything.

Now that we have calmly and sensibly examined

these three excuses—time, money, and folks—we see that each of them melts away as an imaginary obstacle when we shine the light of intelligence upon it. We see that they are not real reasons at all, but merely excuses.

Read the story of any person who has ever achieved his goal, and you will despise yourself for ever yielding to any of these imaginary "time, money, and folks" excuses that may be running through your mind and keeping you from becoming the person you can be.

If you surrender to any of these three excuses, you are destined to mental coma. Failure is certain. The lazy and inefficient use of time, the worship of money, and the futile pursuit of the universal approval of others will distort every worthwhile desire in your heart and rob your life of any personal meaning.

If, on the other hand, you will entirely free your mind from these negative and destructive mental attitudes, you will become completely YOU, and nothing can stop you from doing what you REALLY WANT TO DO.

And the next chapter will show you how to take your first step.

A QUICK RUN-THROUGH OF THIS CHAPTER

✔ 1. Don't postpone your first step toward doing what you want to do. THERE IS NOTHING MAGICAL ABOUT THE FUTURE. The future, when it comes, IS JUST LIKE THE PRESENT.

✔ 2. Begin to build your future TODAY!

✔ 3. TIME, MONEY, AND FOLKS are the three excuses people give for NOT doing what they SAY they want to do. DON'T LET THESE EXCUSES ROB YOUR LIFE OF MEANING!

PART

TWO

HOW TO GO

ABOUT GETTING IT

⑧ TAKE YOUR

FIRST STEP

EVERYONE WHO HAS EVER STUDIED PHYSICS, EVEN IN high school, knows that bodies at rest tend to remain at rest, and bodies in motion tend to remain in motion in the same straight line.

This same fundamental principle also applies to people.

People at rest tend to remain at rest and people in motion tend to remain in motion.

We are all creatures of habit and it takes a certain amount of will power to start doing anything new. However, once you actually get yourself involved, even in a small way, in any new course of action, you tend to continue doing something along those lines and the first thing you know, you're well on your way.

This is the main reason why your FIRST step toward doing what you want to do is so important.

Many people like to read overdramatized stories that tell all about the terrific struggles that somebody or other had to go through before he triumphed over seemingly insurmountable obstacles and reached his goal. And while it is true that nearly everyone must sacrifice something and some may even suffer a little to do what they want, most of the people I know who have accomplished anything unusual did so by taking one undramatic and unspectacular step at a time toward their objective—until they finally arrived at their predetermined destination without much fuss or fanfare at all.

☆ Get Out of the Rut

No matter what you want to do that's new, it's simply a matter of getting out of your big rut for a short time each day, so that you will have a chance to start a small groove in a new direction.

It's no big deal.

It's just a matter of getting yourself involved a little bit *today* instead of tomorrow.

For instance, when Harry McM., the young dress salesman who wanted to be a college professor, took his *first step* by getting the facts concerning how much money he could make as a college teacher and business consultant, this just naturally led to the *second step*—in which he talked the whole thing over with Rose, his wife, and with his father.

These two steps took just a few days.

Then, as soon as Harry had won his father's blessing and his wife's approval, I suggested he go out to the midwestern college from which he had been graduated and talk with some of his former teachers there who thought well of him, to see what the chances were of his getting a part-time job on the campus while he pursued his studies for the doctorate. And this was Harry's *third step*, which he took one week later.

Harry learned, when he made the trip in January, that he could get a part-time job at $3.50 an hour in the Bureau of Business Research at the college and start his graduate study program at the beginning of the second semester in February. He also learned at that time that he could get a half-time job as a research assistant in which he could earn $5,000 a year, beginning the next July. He also found out that Rose, who had been earning $200 a week as an executive secretary in New York before they were married, could make at least $150 a week at a secretarial job on the college campus.

When Harry returned to New York and talked over his findings with Rose, they both decided to move to the college campus.

Two weeks later they made the move, Harry took the job in the Bureau of Business Research and enrolled for the second semester. Rose took a job as secretary in one of the administration offices.

Six months later, Harry landed a half-time job as a research assistant at $500 a month. His marks for the second semester were all in the 90's and Rose was thoroughly enjoying her campus job and the campus life.

One year later, Harry was offered a job as instructor while he continued his graduate work toward the doctorate; and a few months ago, after having been on the campus for about two and a half years, Harry was awarded a predoctoral fellowship by one of the biggest educational foundations in the United States, which pays him $7,000 a year plus free tuition.

Right now, Harry expects to land his Ph.D. degree in one more year. The head of his department—the marketing department—in the Graduate School of Business has told him that he hopes Harry can accept a full-time teaching job as soon as he lands the doctorate.

Incidentally, their first baby has just arrived. It's a boy!

You remember the young secretary Florence Q., who wanted to get married—and wanted to make more money so she could live with two business girl friends in New York so she could be more active socially.

To do this, she realized that she would have to prepare herself for a better job and, since she was very much interested in personnel work, she decided to look into the possibility of taking some evening courses in personnel administration in one of the New York universities.

Her *first step* was to go to the Admissions Office of the university of her choice, where she talked with an advisor who told her that she could take some evening courses in personnel administration as a non-matriculated student, and who recommended a good general course to start with.

This led to her *second step* which was to discuss her program with her employer, who okayed the course as one her company would pay for—in accordance with the company's long-standing policy of paying tuition for night-school courses taken by employees who wished to improve themselves and progress in that company.

Soon after Florence enrolled for the first course, her *next step* was to request a transfer to a secretarial job in the personnel department of her company. Three months later, an opening came up and she was transferred.

As soon as she got into the personnel department, she began to volunteer for various kinds of extra work, when she wasn't busy, just to get better acquainted with what went on in the department—with the result that, in less than a year, she was appointed as a personnel assistant in the women's personnel division of her company, with a nice increase in salary.

Then she found that she was making enough money to help finance a New York apartment with her two business girl friends and that was her next move.

Meanwhile, she met several interesting young men who were also studying personnel administration at the university at night, and one of them turned out to be "Mr. Right."

Two years ago, Florence and Mr. Right were married. Her husband in now employment manager for a grocery chain, and Florence is slated to be the next manager of the women's employment division of her company.

"Even if we start raising a family before that happens," Florence told me, "I feel that I always have something valuable to fall back on if the family ever needs my financial help. And even when I get too old to work for somebody else, I can always open my own employment agency."

Yes, it's remarkable how ONE STEP LEADS TO THE OTHER—when we up and TAKE the FIRST step.

☼ No Matter What Your Age Is, Take That First Step

It's the same story with middle-aged people and older people, too. The first step is the most important.

Remember Thomas D., the middle-aged controller for a canned food company, who wanted to get into the hospital field, and who didn't think he could "make the switch" for "money" reasons? His *first step* was to discuss his desires with a number of hospital authorities whom he had helped as a fund raiser.

His case broke fast.

A month later he wrote me that he had just landed a job as business manager for a New England hospital at approximately the same salary he had been making, and that he was more enthusiastic about his new job than he had ever been in his life. Felt a lot better, too, already.

As Thomas D. told me, "After all, they know I am a good financial administrator, and since one of their main problems is finance, they're glad to have me. Another thing that's mighty important is that in this job I'll be able to adopt more sensible working habits and spend a lot more time with my wife and family."

Now I know very well that a lot of cases, involving middle-aged men who are fed up with what they're doing and would like to switch to another field, do not break so fast.

It is often necessary for a man in this situation with the financial responsibilities of a good-sized family, to effect a *gradual* shift of emphasis from what he is doing to what he thinks he would like to do—carefully weighing each step in advance before he proceeds.

For instance, Irwin T., an air-conditioning sales engineer in Ohio, was fed up with the business and the Middle West in general, and wanted to sell his house, move to Florida, build a home and duplex rental unit there, and get into the real estate business.

However, this was financially risky, for he didn't know how long it might take him to make about the same amount of money a year as he had been making in Ohio.

After thinking the whole thing through, he decided to look into the possibility of setting up a business, similar to his present air-conditioning business, in Florida while he built a home and duplex rental unit and then gradually added other rental units in Florida in due time.

So Irwin T.'s *first step* was to go to Florida and get the facts first hand.

After considerable investigation concerning various types of sales opportunities in his field in Florida, he negotiated with the manufacturer of his choice to represent them there and he was then ready to make the move to Florida without involving himself in too much of a financial risk.

But all this preliminary investigation, exploration, and preparation took several months.

✿ You Can Always Shift Emphasis

Sometimes it takes longer than this to prepare for a desired change—depending on what you're after. But it is always possible for any dissatisfied person to effect a financially safe and gradual shift of emphasis from what he is doing to what he wants to do.

Robert S., a New York mailman, carried the mail for eleven years while he studied part-time to become a clergyman. Now, forty years old, he recently retired as a mailman to become a full-time minister, while he continues his studies toward the Doctor of Divinity degree which he hopes to finish in two more years.

Larry D., a Los Angeles policeman, studied law part-time for nine years before he became a criminal lawyer.

John H., a garage mechanic in a small town in Illinois, was pretty well satisfied with his job until one day he got an emergency call. He arrived at the scene of the accident before the doctor did. Three bodies lay strewn on the road. He knew a lot about fixing automobiles, but he knew nothing about helping these unfortunate people. Soon afterward, this garage mechanic made up his mind to become a physician.

He was married and in his early thirties. *First*, he made up his high school requirements for premedical college at night school while he continued working as a garage mechanic. *Second*, he entered premedical school and pursued his studies during the day while he worked as a "night-call man" at a nearby garage. Meanwhile, his wife took a job in a women's hat shop.

About ten years later, he graduated from medical school, and today he's a country doctor in Illinois, living a full life in a field that's nearer and dearer to him than any other vocation in the world.

And Carrie F., a career woman, finally switched to the job she wanted by beginning with a first step and carrying out a long-range plan.

Nearly forty, she had been a secretary in the New York office of a carpet manufacturer just about all her business life. And she was bored stiff. She made up her mind that she would like to work for a leading woman's magazine and she decided that a promotion writer's job was the one that interested her most.

Her *first step* in that direction was to apply for a secretary's job with that magazine. She was turned down. *Next*, she began to thumb over the magazine every month to find out what companies advertised in its pages so that she could at least try for a secretary's job with one of these companies. Within a short time she landed such a job.

Next, she took some evening courses in advertising and promotion, for one year, and then she put in a request with her company to be transferred to a secretary's job within the promotion department. She got a job as secretary to the assistant promotion manager.

As she learned a little more about advertising and promotion from working in the promotion department and from continuing her evening studies, she began to volunteer for small direct-mail rush jobs which had to go out in a hurry and which everyone else seemed too busy to handle.

Three years after entering this promotion department, she was appointed assistant promotion manager when her boss moved up to the job of promotion manager. She did such a good job of promoting this company's product that her creative efforts came to the attention of the magazine of her dreams. Today, she is one of the top promotion writers for this leading national publication.

☆ Distant Fields Aren't Always Greener

Of course, there are a great many people who only *THINK* they would like to get into another field, largely because distant fields often look greener. Actually, there is nothing the matter with their present job that a little interest on their part wouldn't cure.

Any job can be made more attractive simply by learning to get on congenially with the people you work with. And any job can be made more interesting simply by seeking ways to improve upon what you're doing and looking for some phase of the job that challenges your ingenuity.

As Elbert Hubbard said, "Any man who has a job has a chance."

☆ How To Make a Change

However, if you are thoroughly convinced that your interests lie elsewhere and that you've got to make some kind of switch in order to get into a job that you can get excited about, here is how you can go about making the change, one step at a time.

Step 1.   Test out your desire to get into the new field you are considering by studying this field in your spare time, by talking with some of the people who actually work in it, and by selecting some specific job you either have, or can develop, the ability to fill.

Step 2.   Draw up a plan that will permit a gradual shift of emphasis from what you're doing to what you want to do, so that you can thoroughly prepare yourself for the change.

Step 3.   Prepare yourself for the first job you can hope to hold in your chosen field, and if you cannot make the desired switch within your own organization, select another company that you would be proud to work for. Then talk with some of your friends and find out whether they know someone in that organization well enough so that you can be *favorably introduced* to the *man who can use your services* and *who has the authority to hire you.* When you meet this man, show him why you are interested in his problems and how your services can be used. This means that you should take time to acquaint yourself with that organization and carefully prepare in advance what you are going to say in the interview. If he feels that you can help him, you need not ask him for the job; he will invite you to join his organization. Naturally, the first organization may not be able to use you. But if you are really prepared and see enough prospects, the desired opportunity will come.

Step 4.   Whenever possible, do not leave your present position until you have definitely secured the new job you are after. *An employed person is in a stronger position than one who is out of work.*

Step 5.   Tell your boss that you are contemplating a change. He will appreciate your asking him for advice and taking him into your confidence. Give him the real reasons for your desire to change, so that he will clearly understand that your leaving is no reflection on him or your present position, and that the change is being made merely because you seek an opportunity to get into your chosen field. Ask your boss's advice about approaching any organization which you are interested in negotiating with. He may have some personal contacts that will help you. Even if he hasn't, his suggestions and personal sponsorship will mean a great deal.

Concerning this last step, every now and then somebody will say to me, "My boss isn't the kind of person you can talk things over with." And my reply is, "You can always TRY."

For when it comes to getting a new position, your present boss is the most important sponsor you've got. And you'll probably be a lot better off if you do everything possible to get his support instead of resigning without having made any attempt to take him into your confidence. It's the exceptional boss who does not respond favorably to this kind of treatment. And at least you can have the satisfaction of knowing that you did the right thing in telling him about your plans.

☆ Don't Put Off Making a Switch

The most important point is that if you know you've got to make the switch, don't keep putting it off. Human inertia is a powerful retarding force. And ordinarily we have got to get fired or be mighty uncomfortable before we make a major move of any kind.

When I drove this point home to a man who was dissatisfied with his line of work, he came back with a story which illustrates the point far better than I could.

"When I was a kid back on the farm," he told me, "we had a dog, and like most dogs he liked to lie in front of the fire. It was one of my chores to get up in the morning and start the fires in the kitchen stove and in the fireplace in the dining room. Every morning, our mutt would follow me into the dining room and plant himself about three feet in front of the fireplace. As soon as the fire got started and warmed him up a little, he would fall into a doze. I used to sit there in a chair and watch

him. After a while the logs would begin to throw out
some real heat. But that mutt wouldn't move. Every
now and then he would rouse himself enough to growl
at the fire. Then he'd doze off again. Then he'd growl,
and doze, and growl, and doze. As the fire grew hotter,
he'd growl and *snap* and doze. But not until the fire got
so hot that it almost singed the hair on his starboard
side, would he move back to improve his position.'"

It is unfortunate that most men and women in the
wrong job continue to doze and snap and growl, but
conditions never get quite hot enough to force them to
do anything about it.

But if you feel you ought to change your field, believe
me, it's well worth while to make the move. For when
you're in a job you enjoy, you're more productive, you're
more creative, you feel better, you're easier to get along
with, you live longer, you do a better job, and you enjoy
more of the rewards and pleasures of life.

On the other hand, forcing yourself to work at a job
you dislike is like wearing a lead vest to run a foot race.
It's just plain exhausting!

☼ How Four Persons Took Their First Steps

You will remember that Mary T. lost her husband
and was suddenly faced with the problem of getting a
job and earning enough money to keep her family together until her children were grown up and able to
take care of themselves. It didn't take her very long to
define her desires and to decide that she wanted to
teach English in high school.

Her *first step* was to talk with the local superintend-
ent of schools to find out what she would have to do to
qualify for a teaching job in the local school system.

She learned that, since she was a graduate of a New
England college, she could qualify for a regular teach-

er's job by attending a nearby branch of the state teacher's college for one year. She registered for the fall season and this was her *second step* in the right direction.

To meet her financial problems during that year, Mary decided to use some of the insurance money her husband left her to live on, instead of entirely paying off the mortgage on her home. That fall, she rented a room to a schoolteacher. Her son, who was in high school, got a part-time job as delivery boy for the local drugstore.

Now Mary's son and daughter are both married, while she continues to teach English in high school and rents rooms to young women who come to town as new teachers and who are looking for a comfortable, congenial, inexpensive place to live.

Incidentally, last summer Mary took a trip to Bermuda. On this trip, she met a widower who lives in a nearby town. They've been seeing each other quite often and I wouldn't be one bit surprised if they get married.

Meanwhile, Helen A., who was interested in painting landscapes, took her *first step* in the right direction when she inquired into courses of study which were available and joined a local study group led by an able graduate of one of the leading art schools in the East.

Now she continues her studies in painting with the group, and enters this group's exhibition of paintings once a year in the local Grange hall. Recently she told me that she had sold a couple of paintings for twenty-five dollars each.

Harvey H., the production engineer in upper New York State, who was forced to retire from his job at sixty-five, found, as soon as he began to visit some of the

plants in his area where he was well known and talked
with plant engineers about some of their problems,
that because of the shortage of good engineers he could
apparently "make a pretty good living as a trouble
shooter and engineering consultant."

That was his *first step*.

Today Harvey is offered more work than he can handle, and his earnings this year will be well over what
he needs to live on.

You remember Elsie van M., in her late fifties, whose
children were married, whose husband traveled a lot,
who was lonely, and who suddenly discovered that she
was spending too much time with her married daughter
and that her son-in-law was getting fed up having her
around so much.

As soon as she decided to go in for secretarial work
again, since she had been a top secretary before she was
married, she went to see the personnel director of the
company she had worked for years ago—for she knew
that her former boss had long since retired.

That was Elsie's *first step*.

The personnel director had no immediate opening.
But he did have a good lead.

He told Elsie that the public stenographer in the
same building who did extra work for the company was
always so rushed that she might be glad to get some
help.

Elsie called on the public stenographer and was
hired on the spot—to fill in any hours she could.

Today, Elsie is a new person. She gets a big kick out
of life. She's not lonesome anymore. Now her children
are glad to see her because she's alive and always has
something interesting to contribute to the conversation,
and because she doesn't "drop in" so very often.

Her husband doesn't travel quite so much now.

"Sometimes I think he used to travel just to get away from me because I was such a bore," Elsie told me. "Now even my son-in-law compliments me when I see him. He says he thinks I'm quite a gal. And you know something? *I am!* Now that I've revived my business contacts, I could open up my own public stenographer's office any time I wanted. I've never felt so cocky. I like what I'm doing and, barring any serious mishaps, I've got financial security for a long time to come. It's a wonderful feeling!"

Now, getting back to you, the reader. If you have put your desires down on paper and tested your desires as I suggested, following the simple instructions in Chapter 5 and 6, and if you have succeeded in ridding your mind of the three common excuses for not doing what you want to do—time, money, and folks—which were explained in Chapter 7, you are now ready to TAKE YOUR FIRST STEP toward the realization of YOUR INNER DESIRES.

☼ Get Yourself Involved Today!

No matter what you want out of life, GET YOURSELF INVOLVED TODAY in the FIRST STEP toward getting it. For once you take that first step in the right direction, you will find that each subsequent step is so much easier. In fact, each following step just naturally falls into place.

It's just a matter of finding a little time each day to devote to your new interests instead of worrying about the magnitude of the job ahead.

For instance, suppose I were to ask you to eat a ton of food. No matter how hungry you were, you would balk. Nevertheless, that's what you do eat every year of your life. You can do it because you "nibble" at it every day.

Similarly, by devoting even as little as an hour a day to any goal, you can, little by little, reach it, just as others have.

If you do not believe that you can find even this small amount of time, review *again* a brief outline of what has happened to each hour of the day for the past seven days. Then keep track of what happens to each hour of the next seven days. You will find some free time.

During the small portion of your time that you devote to your new interests, think and act and work just as if you had no other responsibilities whatsoever. This separation of your life into two parts will do an interesting thing: It will clear your thinking. It will free you from the muddling effects of attempting to think of a number of things at the same time. It will protect you from the feeling of futility because it will free your mind from destructive objections that always come to you when you think of your present responsibilities.

It will do another important thing. It will help you to shift emphasis from your present responsibilities. It will make them appear smaller to you, whereas if you do nothing but think of your present burdens, they become bigger than you—they rule you.

Even though most of your time, for the present, must be devoted to your present responsibilities, it is perfectly foolish for you to think that you must give up changing your life for the better.

And no matter how much or how little of your time is involved in your first step, the most important fundamental for you to remember is to exercise the necessary patience to begin at the beginning and to lead an orderly, systematic, irresistible advance, one step at a time, toward your inevitable goal.

☼ Set Up a Definite Schedule for Your New Interest

However small your first step in the direction of your new interest, however little the time required to accomplish it, a *definite schedule* will make the job easier and more certain of achievement.

In fact, if you do not provide a definite place in your daily life for your new interest, it will be postponed, kicked around, finally ignored and forgotten.

Without a schedule for our free time, we waste much of it wondering what we ought to do—trying to select something out of a maze of duties or pleasures that happen to capture the attention of our roving mind. Our mental machinery becomes so exhausted with the task of selection that sometimes we do nothing at all.

A schedule eliminates this waste motion. Give your first step a certain time in your daily schedule, and when that time comes, begin work on it.

"But what about interruptions?" you say.

Women are interrupted when someone comes to the door, or when the phone rings, or when a child needs attention, or when their husbands yell for missing tools. And men may be interrupted by things like this, too, when they are at home.

LET'S FACE IT: *You're going to be interrupted.* But the regularity of a schedule assures that you work on your new interests often enough so that even with interruptions, you are able to get somewhere in the long run. And after all, it's better to be interrupted from doing something worth while than from doing nothing.

☼ Make Your Schedule EASY TO MEET

Many schedules for self-improvement are made. But few are followed. The main reason is that they are too tight, too difficult to follow. They are built up in a moment of great enthusiasm and they fall of their own dead weight under everyday circumstances.

So make your schedule *easy to meet*.

First, make your schedule light. Don't try to schedule *all* your spare time. If, for example, you have a full-time job, an hour every other evening, with a couple of hours on Saturday or Sunday, will average four or five hours a week. To begin with, this might be enough of your spare time to schedule. And if you're a housewife, raising a family, four or five hours a week might be enough for you, too.

Second, schedule a time of the day or night when other matters are least likely to interfere.

Third, schedule a time of the day or night when you find yourself best able to perform the work which your schedule requires.

Now, THIS IS IMPORTANT! *Consider these hourly appointments with yourself just as important as an appointment with another person!*

No matter what is involved in your first step—reading up on your chosen field, talking with people who work in this field, writing to educational leaders or other authorities in your field, or taking a course of study—if you get yourself *involved today* in thinking about what your first step should be, and if you provide scheduled times in your day or week to work at your interest, the first step will lead to the following steps so easily that your progress will become automatic.

✿ WARNING: Don't Talk Away Your Enthusiasm!

Once you decide on your fist step, don't make the common mistake of talking away your enthusiasm by telling everybody your plans and by bragging about what you are going to do.

Confine your conversations to those who are in a position to help you.

Just remember that any time you get a new idea, your initial impulse is to tell all your friends and associates about your plans—what you are going to do, what you are ultimately going to be.

Squash that impulse!

Whenever you broadcast your plans here, there, and everywhere, you expose yourself on the one hand to those who ease you along with meaningless and uninformed approval, and on the other hand to those who can think up a dozen reasons why you are an imbecile for considering such a goal.

Some kind friends are bound to offer criticisms and objections to your program that, in the beginning, you are too inexperienced to answer. They will paint pictures of hardship that will make you afraid.

No matter what new project a man or woman attempts, there is always a crop of gapers ready to laugh or to criticize. And sometimes those nearest and dearest may laugh the loudest or criticize the most.

So instead of squandering your early enthusiasm in a futile attempt to excite the world about you and your plans, preserve that enthusiasm within yourself. Instead of letting your enthusiasm flow out through your mouth like a weak shallow creek, dam it up. Let it accumulate and gradually gain the power of a deep reservoir. That power will give you the necessary confidence to get started on your first step.

✧ How to Gain Confidence and Courage

Confidence is difficult to define. But I can give you an excellent example of it.

When I was at the University of Chicago, my days

were full. But I spent half an hour every evening from 5:30 to 6:00 in the university swimming pool. One afternoon I was in the locker-room, getting undressed, and I noticed that my neighbor was a blind man who was also preparing for a swim.

"Will you take me in to the swimming pool?" he asked. "This is my first visit to your Chicago pool."

"Be glad to," I answered, and we walked toward the pool.

"Now you are at the side of the pool," I told him, "and this is the shallow end. Shall I help you in?"

"Oh no!" he laughed. "Take me to the deep end. I like to dive!"

This confidence startled me, but I took him to the edge of the pool at the deep end, and he asked, "How far is the water level below us?"

My hair raised just a little. "About two feet below where we're standing."

"Is there anybody in the way?"

"No, it's all right to dive now." And before I had finished speaking he had made one of the prettiest dives I have ever seen.

When the time comes for you to dive into the pool of your new interests, you must have that kind of confidence. And don't be disappointed if your first dive results in a belly-flopper. No matter how many times you fall flat, you must have the intelligence to study and to correct your mistakes, and you must have the courage to get up on the board and try it again.

As Sydney Smith wrote, "A great deal of talent is lost in the world for want of a little courage. Every day sends to their graves obscure men whom timidity prevented from making a first effort; who, if they could have been induced to begin, would in all probability have gone great lengths in the career of fame. The fact is, that to do anything in the world worth doing, we must not stand back shivering and thinking of the cold and danger, but jump in and scramble through as well as we can."

THIS CHAPTER—IN A NUTSHELL

✔ 1. Remember that bodies at rest tend to remain at rest, and that bodies in motion tend to remain in motion. THIS MEANS YOU, TOO.

✔ 2. Your FIRST STEP toward doing what you want to do is your MOST IMPORTANT STEP; the next steps just naturally follow.

✔ 3. GET YOURSELF INVOLVED TODAY in THINKING about your first step.

✔ 4. SCHEDULE A SPECIFIC TIME for your new interest, so that it doesn't get kicked around and forgotten.

✔ 5. Consider this time JUST AS IMPORTANT AS A DATE WITH ANOTHER PERSON.

✔ 6. DON'T TALK AWAY YOUR ENTHUSIASM!

✔ 7. You've got to have enough CONFIDENCE AND COURAGE TO TAKE THAT FIRST DIVE.

9

HOW TO MAKE UP
YOUR MIND
AND BE RIGHT

IT IS QUITE NATURAL FOR US TO TAKE FOR GRANTED
our *own* ability to think straight. We would like to believe, and, for the most part, do believe that we are fair
and open-minded. Although we can often see that the
conclusions of another person are foolish, prejudiced, or
one-sided, each of us is inclined to feel that his own
thinking is pretty reasonable.

However, anyone who will take the time and exercise
the patience necessary to review and to analyze his own
thought processes, as well as those of other people, will
soon find out that the everyday thinking of most of us is
not very orderly and not very sound.

116

☆ Use Orderly Thinking

Now obviously, when a person knows how to think straight and arrive at sound solutions to his everyday problems, he has a much better chance of getting what he wants out of life than the person who just "muddles through."

Actually, there is no mystery about the scientific method for solving problems.[1] No matter what the problem, there are four traditional steps which scientific workers in every field accept and follow. Stated in simple terms, these four steps are:

➠*Step 1.* Separate facts from opinions and analyze the facts from the standpoint of who, what, when, and where.

➠*Step 2.* Define the *real* problem and consider possible solutions.

➠*Step 3.* Secure evidence on possible solutions.

➠*Step 4.* Weigh the advantages and disadvantages of each possible solution and arrive at a sound conclusion.

But is this the way we think?

Not by a long shot.

Psychologists have been telling us for a good many years now that we get most of our mental exercise by jumping to conclusions.

And this is true.

☆ How Our Minds Jump

There is nothing more common than a husband who looks over the family financial situation and who jumps

---

[1] William J. Reilly, *The Twelve Rules for Straight Thinking—Applied to Business and Personal Problems.* New York: Harper & Brothers, 1947.

to the conclusion that his wife is getting extravagant with his money. And this is exactly what happened to Jim T.

"You used to be more careful with our money," he told his wife, Grace. "We used to get along on $500 a month and save a little too. Now I'm making a lot more and we're further behind than we ever were. No matter how much money I made, you'd have it spent before I got it! Believe me, you've *got* to stop being so extravagant!"

After the smoke of battle had cleared away and Grace had gotten over her crying spell, it began to dawn on Jim that maybe he was a little hasty in blaming it all on the little woman. After all, the children were growing up and needing more things, they were living in a nicer house than they used to, they were doing more entertaining than they had, and he himself was playing more golf at the club and smoking better cigars.

Outside the home, we are more likely to be on guard in our thinking. But the moment we cross the threshold of home sweet home, we are inclined to let ourselves go. In fact, we unconsciously act as if all our mistakes should be accepted with perfect understanding and that all members of the family just naturally ought to love each other regardless.

☆ Jumping to Conclusions at Home

But the facts of life show that this is not so. They show that members of our own family can get just as angry as anyone else. And some of the hasty, thoughtless, cutting remarks made around the house can, and sometimes do, start big family wars and result in more downright unhappiness than all our "outside" mistakes put together.

It's not only the husband who makes cracks about his wife's being extravagant, instead of carefully examining the family budget to find out how expenses can be reduced. It's the wife who gives her husband the business for being out late before he's even had a chance to explain; the mother who snaps "No!" to many of the things her children ask for, when she could just as well say "Yes"; the father who rides his children for every little misstep instead of trying, through quiet and properly timed discussion, to understand why they acted as they did.

If husbands and wives could only learn how to hold their fire, the divorce rate wouldn't be so high. And if parents could only learn to hold their fire, their children would respect them more.

None of us is perfect. Every day in the week, at home and abroad, we jump to some fast conclusion and are tempted to say something we later wish we hadn't.

But even when you do forget and take a verbal swing at someone, you've still got an "out" if you're brave enough to use it. *You can apologize as quickly as possible.* This will take much of the sting out of your mistake. It will make you feel better. It's the next best thing to holding your fire in the first place.

☆ How Disorderly Thinking Blocks Problem-solving

Sometimes a "problem" never gets past the first step in straight thinking.

Jane R.'s mother, living in Philadelphia, was to have a serious operation. Jane wrote her brother in Oregon and told him it would be performed in about ten days.

When her mother went to the hospital, Jane had not heard from her brother. But all through the difficult time, just before and after the operation, Jane expected to see some flowers or at least some kind of message from her brother. None came. And Jane got madder and madder.

Finally, two days after the operation, Jane called her brother long-distance and told him off. It wasn't until Jane started crying that her amazed brother had a chance to tell her that he had had a letter from his mother saying that the proposed operation had been postponed for a month. Apparently his mother just didn't want him to worry about her, that's all.

Lots of times we find that a "problem" disappears in thin air once the facts come to light and it becomes apparent that we were fighting a "ghost." In fact, you never know whether you've got a *real* problem or not, until you dig into the facts.

Everyone who works for a living is in danger of jumping to conclusions on problems before the facts are in. I know an able sales manager who, observing a lot of mistakes in a salesman's reports, jumped to the conclusion that "this guy's getting entirely too careless. He must be drunk half the time to write reports like this. I think we ought to get rid of him."

It wasn't until after the man had been fired that the sales manager learned this salesman was gradually going blind and had been dictating his reports to a public stenographer who made frequent errors because she was not familiar with the technical language of the business, and that these errors were never picked up because he was unable to read the reports back. Then the sales manager immediately apologized and re-hired the man.

But many costly business mistakes are never found out until it's much too late to correct them. Perrin Stryker, writing for *Fortune* magazine,[1] quoted one leading businessman as saying: "The number and cost of undiscovered $10,000 mistakes made in our company

---

[1] Perrin Stryker, "Can Executives Be Taught To Think?" *Fortune*, May, 1953.

as a result of faulty thinking are more staggering than anyone would wish to contemplate."

And everyone who runs any kind of big business would readily admit this.

In business conferences, it's common to have someone pop off with a premature conclusion, because he wants to seem well informed or maybe because he wants to make a star play.

Someone calls a business meeting on the spur of the moment and the top men have their say first.

Now here's George, an assistant manager of some department or other, seated down toward the end of the table. The "gassing" has been going on for thirty or forty minutes, and George's mind has begun to wander. He may be thinking of last night when he was playing with his little boy in the front room and barked his shin.

"Gosh! That thing is beginning to hurt a little," he says to himself as he casually adjusts his garter with one hand under the table. "Huh! Right under the garter!"

Just then the leader of the meeting says, "What do *you* think of this, George?"

George's ears fly up as he shakes himself out of the trance.

"Why—well, I'll tell you, Mr. Johnson, I don't like the color of it. It's too yellow. Frankly, it—it doesn't look right to me."

Now the damage has been done! George has committed himself to an opinion. From that moment on, therefore, he begins to spend the company's time and money in an opportunistic pursuit of any or all kinds of evidence that will support the wisdom of this halfbaked opinion which he has expressed on the spur of the moment.

This costs money in business. In fact, business is full of feuds and disagreements arising from such ill-considered opinions.

There would be far less expensive conclusion-jumping in business meetings if, whenever possible, meetings, together with their *specific purpose*, were announced a week in advance, and if everyone invited to sit in were told what part he would have in the meeting and what facts he should gather in advance.

But there's just no getting away from it—all of us are guilty of conclusion-jumping on the basis of inadequate evidence at some time or another.

It even happened to the Chief Justice of the Supreme Court of the United States.

On election night, 1916, Charles Evans Hughes retired, believing himself the next President of the United States. A little after midnight a newspaperman called to tell him that California was in doubt.

"The President cannot be disturbed," announced young Charles Hughes, Jr.

The newspaperman persisted.

"You will have to come back in the morning; the President cannot be disturbed."

"Well, when he wakes up, just tell him he isn't President," the reporter replied.[1]

☼ How We Arrive at Decisions by Default

The other main way in which we arrive at decisions, without really thinking at all, is by *default*.

It's the *disagreeable* decisions that we especially like to postpone. But when we postpone a decision, *we really make one*.

When you put off a trip to the dentist, it is a decision to let the tooth get worse. A person with a toothache

---

[1] Drew Pearson and Robert S. Allen, *The Nine Old Men*.

would say you were crazy if you told him that he had actually *decided* to have that toothache. But that is exactly what he did when he postponed his trip to the dentist.

When a woman puts off "doing anything" about reducing her figure, it's the same as if she decided to stay as fat as she is.

When a young man postpones a decision to enroll in that night school course he's been talking about, it is a decision not to make this effort to improve himself.

The main reason why most men and women reach the later years without having anything interesting to do with themselves, is that, in their prime, they put off making any provision for the later years and thereby decided, without fully realizing it, to spend their declining years in boredom.

Just look back on your week and you'll probably find some decisions that you have arrived at by default.

✫ *How We Ought To Think*

Let's get one thing straight at the very outset concerning how we ought to think. We cannot possibly *stop* our minds from jumping to conclusions. The mind of man has been jumping in this way for so many thousands of years that you cannot hope to stop it entirely.

In our emotional desire to capture the spotlight in our social conversations, in our attempts to make an impression on the boss, or in our eagerness to prove that we are men or women of action who can make sound decisions quickly, we are continually tempted to jump to a hasty decision and make the mistake of offering some quick answer instead of taking plenty of time to think things through.

The big trouble is that most of us easily mistake a quick solution as the best solution or the only solution, whereas a quick solution is all too often a poor one and may often be the wrong one which doesn't solve the problem at all, but only creates a lot of new problems. In fact, it's surprising how many of our problems we ourselves actually create by conclusion jumping.

While you *cannot stop* your mind from jumping, you can *know* it jumps. And you can *protect yourself* from the damaging effects of conclusion-jumping by using the DELAYED RESPONSE to any problem; i.e., giving yourself sufficient time to think it through, as you should.

After all, the *delayed response* is the first sign of intelligence—the first sign of thought. In fact, any time a person comes to you with a problem and you say, "Let me think about this. I don't trust myself on quick decisions on important matters," you are bound to make a favorable impression on that person.

This delayed response will give your mind the necessary time to think—to back up and go through the four simple steps in straight thinking. Remember this: *It's far better to take four steps and be sure, than to take one jump and be sorry.*

✿ Step 1. Separate Facts From Opinions and Analyze the Facts

Straight thinking starts with facts. Careless thinking starts with opinion. And every day of our lives we mix them up without realizing it.

If you were to begin today to form the mental habit of listening carefully to the statements you hear in the course of your conversations with friends and associates, you would be utterly amazed at the high percentage of such statements which are without adequate foundation. Many of the statements are merely opinions. Even when facts are included, they are often loosely combined with opinions or impressions—clearly demonstrating that the person making the statement has made no conscious effort to *discriminate* between the two.

For example, let's listen again to what Jim T. said to his wife, Grace, when he accused her of being extravagant with his money:

"You used to be more careful with our money. We used to get along on $500 a month and save a little too. Now I'm making a lot more and we're further behind than we ever were. No matter how much money I made, you'd have it spent before I got it. Believe me, you've *got* to stop being so extravagant!"

Separating *fact* from *opinion* in this statement:

FACT	OPINION
1. We used to get along on $500 a month and save a little too.	1. You used to be more careful with our money.
2. Now I'm making a lot more and we're further behind than we ever were.	2. No matter how much money I made, you'd have it spent before I got it.
	3. Believe me, you've got to stop being so extravagant.

Jim could have avoided the nasty quarrel with his wife if *he* had separated fact from opinion. For then he would have looked at the above facts, seen that the only one that needed analysis was Fact No. 2. And once he had analyzed the facts on WHAT the money was being spent for, WHEN it was being spent, WHERE it was being spent, and for WHOM, he would have been in a well-informed position to discuss with Grace their *real problem* of trying to cut expenses. Then they could have calmly discussed VARIOUS POSSIBLE SOLUTIONS for cutting down a little here and there, and they could have arrived at the BEST PLAN for balancing their budget.

Or take the case of Thelma G., whose wallet disappeared from the hall table, and who jumped to the conclusion that the television repairman, who had just left, had taken it.

Highly excited, she phoned the service company, and here's what she said:

"I missed my wallet right after he left. It was right there on the hall table. He must have picked it up on his way out. He was the only one who was in the house. There's $20 in that wallet and I want it back . . . quick!"

She had hardly hung up the phone when her little girl, aged three, walked into the room with the wallet in her hand. "Look, Mommy, I'm playing store!"

Obviously Thelma could have saved herself this embarrassing mistake if she had (1) separated fact from opinion when she first missed the wallet; and (2) analyzed the facts from the standpoint of WHO, WHAT, WHEN, and WHERE. For when she came to "WHO" was around, she would have included her little girl too as a possible suspect.

It is impossible for us to have an accurate understanding of any problem unless we SEPARATE FACT FROM OPINION and ANALYZE THE FACTS from the standpoint of WHO, WHAT, WHEN, and WHERE. To start out with any kind of unsupported opinion results either in our misconception of the real problem or in the futile pursuit of a solution to a problem which doesn't even exist.

So, no matter what kind of problem you face—personal, business, or otherwise—if you will start your thinking by SEPARATING FACT FROM OPINION and ANALYZE THE FACTS from the standpoint of WHO, WHAT, WHEN, and WHERE, you will immediately begin to boost your batting average on SOUND DECISIONS. For you will be taking the first big step toward overcoming the human tendency we all have of jumping from opinion to premature conclusion without really thinking at all.

☆ Step 2. Define Your REAL Problem and Consider Possible Solutions

As we have already found out, some of our so-called problems are not "for real." And when we break down the facts, the problem disappears into thin air.

But if the problem *is* "for real," you're able to see it in clearer relief when you analyze the facts.

Let's be aware, though, that many of the so-called problems which arise in the usual course of everyday conversations, are not to be looked upon as problems at all.

For instance, some sweet young thing says: "I don't know *what* to do. I've had this date with George for tonight and Tom is in from New Haven. I just *can't* make any excuses to Tom, and yet I wouldn't offend George for the world. What would you do?"

This young lady doesn't *really* want your help on a problem. What she's really trying to do is impress you with her popularity, and for you to come right out with a simple solution would be disappointing indeed.

Or some big business executive tells you that he's been *so busy* with so many important deals that he hasn't been home for dinner all week and laughingly comments: "My wife and children hardly know me any more. I haven't even been out on my boat for almost *ten days!* And I'm drinking too much, too. How do you manage to look so fit all the time, Joe? You don't seem to be so busy. How do you do it?"

This executive doesn't want your help any more than the sweet young thing does. He just thinks "busy-ness" is the hallmark of a big business executive. And he wants you to know he's got a boat.

So the safest thing to say in all such instances is, "My, oh my, I don't see how you do it!"

Or, if you're not allotted enough time to say all this, just listen attentively and say, "My, oh my!"

☼ Some Real Problems

Now let's get down to the definition of some REAL problems.

When it comes to defining real problems, the main pitfall to look out for is this: *We are inclined to take the first possible solution that happens to pop into our minds, and make the mistake of thinking THAT'S our problem.*

The result is that we not only work on the *wrong* problem, but we overlook the REAL problem and do not give ourselves a chance to consider *all possible solutions to the REAL problem.*

This is what happened to the woman who missed her wallet. She thought that her problem was to get the wallet back from the service man, and she worked on that, to her sorrow.

And Jim T. thought that his problem was to get his wife, Grace, to stop being so extravagant. So he got into a nasty argument and they both said a lot of things they didn't mean. Whereas, the *real* problem in this case was for both Jim and Grace to get together and balance the budget by thinking up various possible cuts in expenses.

When Louis D. came to me, following a series of quarrels with his wife, Jean, he wanted to know if I could recommend a good lawyer who knew the different ways in which residents of New Jersey could get a divorce.

"Louis, I'm not a marriage counselor," I told him.

"But I do know something about straight thinking. And it seems to me that you are *thinking only in terms of one possible solution* to your problem. Isn't it true that your real problem is what you ought to do about your unfortunate relations with your wife and that divorce is only one possible solution?"—to which Louis finally, if somewhat reluctantly, agreed.

We'll get back to Louis in the next step.

☼ *Career Problems*

When it comes to career problems, here again we often mistake one possible solution to our problem for the real problem, and we thereby restrict our thinking.

For instance, a young man Allan T. recently came to me and said, "My problem is to get a job with a leading New York advertising agency. Can you give me any leads?"

As a matter of fact, this represented only one possible solution to his problem, which was "what kind of job should I go after in light of my interests in the field of advertising, my ability to sell, and my desire to associate with leaders in the field from whom I can get some salable experience?"

Obviously, this statement of his real problem opened his eyes to a number of possible solutions. He began to consider other possible markets for his services among manufacturers, retailers, publishers of newspapers or magazines, radio or television stations, outdoor advertising companies, printers, and other types of organizations involved in the creation and sale of advertising.

And he finally came up with three possible solutions that interested him most:

1) Some kind of job with a leading New York advertising agency.

2) A job selling advertising for a newspaper, magazine, radio or TV station.

3) A job in the advertising department of a national
manufacturer.

Similarly, if you're a housewife seeking some outside
interest, be sure to frame the statement of your real
problem as, "What kind of outside interests would fit
my desires, my abilities, and my facility in human relations?" instead of restricting yourself to the first possible solution that happens to pop into your mind.

If you want to get married, you don't pick the first
person who comes along; and if you're sick, you don't
pick the first doctor listed in the telephone book.

So the next time you face any kind of important problem, just ask yourself whether you are restricting your
thinking to one possible solution to your problem.

And if you are, just *broaden out* the statement of
your problem, similar to the examples which have been
given. Then you will begin to think of other possible
solutions which are available to you.

☆ Step 3. Secure Evidence on Possible Solutions

Even though you define your real problem and thoroughly consider the various possible solutions, if your
collection of evidence on various solutions is biased,
your conclusion will be nothing but the product of a prejudiced mind.

Many of our everyday problems, of course, do not
permit the time for, or are not of sufficient importance to
justify any extended pursuit of evidence.

But no matter how little or how much evidence we
gather on any problem, we often find that we have certain preconceptions or prejudices that interfere with our
impartial reception of that evidence.

As the authors of a book called *Our Changing Social*

Order[1] wrote concerning the difficulty of straight thinking: "To think STRAIGHT about either a personal or a social problem is far from easy. Our feelings get in the way, and we let our wishes shape our conclusions. Then, too, we often make up our minds before we get the facts, or we take the facts from unreliable sources. All of us can learn, however, to think better than we do."

How eagerly we welcome with open arms any kind of evidence that supports our pet solution to a problem, or that agrees with opinions we have openly expressed! And how blind we are to evidence that contradicts our preconceptions! Or if someone makes himself disagreeable by calling such unwelcome evidence to our attention, how antagonistic and inhospitable we are in our reception!

Therefore, we must make a sincere effort to open our minds to evidence for or against any possible solution to the problem—whether it supports our pet solution or not.

For example, to get back to Louis D., who wanted a divorce. Even though he did admit that divorce was only one possible solution to his present difficulty with his wife, he still continued to repeat to me all the things that were *wrong* with his wife.

"Look, Louis," I said. "If anyone put down on paper all the things that are wrong with me, they would wind up with a pretty long list. And if anyone deliberately tried to think of all the things that are wrong with you, they might build a good list, too.

"You've been telling me everything that's *wrong* with your wife. Why don't you try this? Put down on paper some of the reasons you married her in the first place. Put down all her *good* points.

---

[1] Ruth W. Gavian, A. A. Gray, and Ernest R. Groves, *Our Changing Social Order*.

"For instance, she hasn't tried to poison you yet, has she?" I asked lightly.

"No," Louis laughed. "Not yet."

"Well . . . that's GOOD. Put that down first," I smiled. "And then follow with everything you can think of that's RIGHT about her. Maybe you'll build up enough evidence to stay married to Jean. And don't forget this, if you do get a divorce and marry someone else, it will take you several years to find out what's wrong with *her*. You already know what's wrong with Jean. Think the whole thing through and come back in a few days and we'll talk some more."

☆ Build People Up

Too many married couples make the mistake of tearing each other down—looking for weaknesses and imperfections.

Every time I see a young couple married, I feel like telling both of them—and I often do—"Your most important job from now on is to keep building each other up."

As Katherine Fullerton Gerould once wrote: "Nothing makes people so worthy of compliments as occasionally receiving them. One is more delightful for being told one is delightful—just as one is more angry for being told one is angry."

And as Mark Twain said, "I can live for two months on a good compliment."

When parents get into the habit of building each other up instead of tearing each other down, they favorably affect the whole atmosphere of a home. And if parents go one step further and build their children up instead of tearing them down, the children will also respond with a smile.

Children are SO HUNGRY for love and approval—

just as hungry as adults are—and if you EXPRESS your love and approval whenever you get a chance, they'll love you for it and they'll build YOU up.

It's a good idea—at home and abroad—to accept people as they are. Don't expect them to be *perfect*. *Expect* them to make some mistakes. And don't jump all over them when they do.

Just build people up, that's all. Don't tear them down. And they'll respond by being better people. All of us would have fewer "people" problems if we did not create some of these problems ourselves by tearing other people down.

☆ Collect the Evidence

Let's return to the career problem of Allan T., who was interested in the field of advertising. He too had a pet solution: getting a job with a leading advertising agency. And when he called on one of the big New York agencies, he found he could get a job in the research department.

He liked the whole atmosphere of the agency's swanky offices, he liked the people he met there, and he liked the director of research who took him to lunch at a college club. In fact, it seemed to him that his career problem was just about solved. However, after he had called on some national manufacturers and found that some of them offered well-rounded training programs for college graduates in their advertising departments, and after he had called on some advertising media and learned that he could get a job selling classified advertising for one of the biggest newspapers in the New York area, and after he had called on some department stores and learned about the possibilities of approaching the field of advertising from the retail angle, he was thoroughly convinced that the business of arriving at the best possible solution to his problem deserved careful study.

No matter what your problem may be, if it's an important problem, don't make the mistake of jumping to any fast conclusion while you are still in the process of collecting evidence. Don't be in a hurry to make up your mind. Don't permit some sudden burst of enthusiasm to make you impatient. No matter how certain you are that you have hit on the right solution, keep your mind open until you have finished collecting evidence for and against each possible solution you have listed.

In collecting your evidence, it is wise to confine yourself to information that is gathered from responsible people who have no axe to grind and from authoritative sources. Don't discuss your possible solutions with friends or associates unless they have some factual information which they can contribute to the study of your problem. And don't pay any attention to printed information unless it comes from a reliable source.

If you feel the need of personal counsel, go to an authority who has no personal interest in your decision, except that it be a sound one.

✡ *Step 4. Weigh the Evidence and Arrive at a Sound Conclusion*

As soon as you know how to arrive at sound decisions, you are well on the way toward getting the money, love, and ego food that you want out of life, and you are just bound to spare yourself much of the worry and mental torture that upsets your nerves, ruins your digestion, robs you of sleep, and in general tears down your health.

Life presents one problem after another, each of which demands a decision. Yet so many of the questions which we let upset us and ruin our disposition are really of small consequence. The trouble is we just don't realize it at the time.

You know the woman who worries all day about what she's going to have for the evening meal. Can't make up her mind until the last minute. Then if she and her husband are going out to play bridge that night, she can't decide whether she should just wear what she's got on or put on that gray suit.

You know men, too, who are real fussbudgets. They study a menu until the waitress is ready to scream, before they finally select "apple pie." Or they hold a full-scale debate on whether or not to shave before they go over to the Jones's for the evening. They never get far, no matter what they work at. They need someone to make their decisions for them and that someone is usually the boss or the wife.

You've heard parents get into a prolonged hassle with their children about something that makes very little difference. After all, what difference does it make if Junior sends twenty-five cents and a boxtop to the cereal company because he wants to get that new space ship, or whether little Mary takes her new green sweater or her old blue sweater to camp?

And what difference does it make if you have to wait for your wife or your husband for ten or fifteen minutes when you're going out somewhere?

People get into more doggoned arguments about little things around the home. In fact, it's usually the little *un*important matters that start big family wars.

☼ The Important vs. the Trivial

If you want to learn how to make up your mind with a maximum of wisdom and a minimum of wear and tear on your mental apparatus, *learn to distinguish between what's important and what isn't.*

If a problem is relatively unimportant, you can arrive at a quick decision with the simple assurance that it doesn't make much difference which way your decision falls.

One of the simplest ways to go about separating what's important from what isn't, is to develop your *own* standards in relation to:

➤➤Money.
➤➤Time.
➤➤People.

Concerning *money*, you might decide right now that any decision involving less than one dollar, two dollars, five dollars, or even ten dollars or more, is a relatively unimportant matter. And once you set your standard, you can make fast decisions on expenditures under that amount.

My standard on money is five dollars. Any decision that involves less than five dollars, I classify as relatively unimportant, and I can appear to be positively brilliant in arriving at a quick decision. On a problem like this, I've got a mind like a steel trap.

For instance, the other morning when I arrived at the Midway Airport in Chicago and wanted to get to the Edgewater Beach Hotel on the North Shore, I found the airlines limousine waiting outside to take passengers downtown, and a taxicab just behind it.

Which should I take?

The regular airline limousine would have cost me about $14 to get downtown, and then I knew that a cab to the Edgewater Beach Hotel would have cost me another few dollars, while I estimated that a cab from the airport to the hotel might cost me around twenty dollars.

So I made a quick decision and immediately stepped

into the cab because the *difference* in the cost was less than five dollars.

Now I could have stood there, separated fact from opinion, analyzed the facts from the standpoint of *who, what, when,* and *where,* defined my real problem and considered possible solutions, secured evidence on various possible solutions from authoritative sources, weighed the evidence for and against each possible solution and arrived at a sound conclusion concerning my best course of action.

BUT I might *still* be standing out there at the Midway Airport!

Concerning *time,* I merely ask myself, "What difference will it make one year from now?" If my answer is "No difference," I usually classify the problem at hand as relatively unimportant.

Concerning *people,* I ask myself, "Will it hurt anyone?" If my decision will hurt anyone, it suddenly becomes a very important decision to me. For I can't afford to hurt anyone. I need everybody.

Once you set your own personal standards for separating what's important from what isn't—in relation to money, time, and people—and once you get into the habit of making quick decisions on relatively unimportant matters, you will soon get the reputation for being brilliant. You don't have to tell people *why* you appear so brilliant.

This simple separation of what's important from what isn't will do much to eliminate the petty arguments that make mountains out of molehills at home and abroad. It's far easier to give in to your sweetheart, your boss, your children, your neighbor, or your dog, when you realize that the whole matter doesn't amount to a hill of beans. It will help you if you will remember that you are no bigger than the things which upset you.

However, when a problem IS important, it deserves careful study from *all angles*. And you will want to take as much time as you are allowed, in order to weigh the evidence for and against each possible solution to your problem.

✡ *Balance Sheets*

The simplest way to study a problem is to set up a balance sheet on each possible solution. Just draw a line down a blank piece of paper and put your advantages on the right-hand side and your disadvantages on the left-hand side.

There are two important reasons for using balance sheets on important problems.

In the first place, *balance sheets assure you that ALL the evidence you have at hand will be brought to bear on your conclusion rather than only part of it.*

Without the aid of balance sheets, you will find yourself tormented with all kinds of random thoughts, some favoring a decision one way, others pointing in the opposite direction. Certain bits of evidence will come to your mind again and again; and your decision will be swayed one way and then the other, depending on what bit of evidence is in your mind at the time. And after you get mentally sick and tired of the whole business, you will finally reach a decision at the last moment, when you are forced to do so under pressure, and your decision will be dictated by that part of the evidence which happens to be foremost in your mind when you get tired of thinking.

Then, after you have made your decision, you'll begin to wonder whether you did the right thing because things will come to your mind which you knew all the time, but which you just didn't remember in time.

In the second place, *balance sheets permit a quick and well-rounded view of the advantages and disadvantages of each possible solution.*

There are always certain advantages that must be sacrificed no matter which way you make your decision, so unless you use balance sheets your problem is likely to be left hanging in the air. Your mind will be haunted first by the disadvantages of deciding one way and then by the disadvantages of deciding the other way. In such a mental condition, it is difficult for you to make up your mind because you do not see ALL the advantages and disadvantages in their PROPER BALANCE. And there is nothing that exacts such a heavy toll on your mental efficiency as the inability to reach a decision.

In fact, it is this inability to reach a decision that causes most of our mental disturbances and that has been identified by psychologists as the primary cause for suicide.

With the use of a balance sheet, however, you will be able to survey advantages and disadvantages at a glance, reach your decision, and spare yourself the mental torment that comes from excessive deliberation.

Balance sheets will help to keep you from being over-optimistic or over-pessimistic. Optimists are inclined to see points *in favor* of doing something, and are apt to *overlook the points against doing it.* Pessimists are inclined to do just the opposite.

Now you don't want to be either over-optimistic or over-pessimistic. You want to be *realistic.* You want to see *both sides* of every possible solution.

Finally, an important point to keep in mind in arriving at any decision is that when it comes to human problems, THERE ARE NO PERFECT ANSWERS.

We are all imperfect. The people we live with and work with and associate with in any way whatsoever are all imperfect.

Remember! One of the first signs of maturity in anyone is *his capacity to live with an imperfect solution to a human problem!*

If more men and women understood this one simple fact of life, perhaps our divorce rate would not be so high.

After Louis D. had gathered evidence on the possible solutions to his unfortunate relations with his wife, he set up the two following balance sheets:

POSSIBLE SOLUTION NO. 1— IF I DIVORCE MY WIFE

DISADVANTAGES	ADVANTAGES
1. I love my children very much and I'm afraid this would hurt them in many ways.	1. I'd get away from this nasty situation at home.
2. It would cost me important money because I'd have to pay alimony and if I married again I might have a tough time financing it.	2. Then I could try to marry someone I could get along with better.
3. Jean does have a lot of good points and I could do worse. After all, I don't know what might be the matter with the next girl I'd marry.	

POSSIBLE SOLUTION NO. 2—
IF I DON'T DIVORCE MY WIFE

DISADVANTAGES	ADVANTAGES
1. I certainly can't stand this running battle at home for very much longer. My work is suffering. I can't even concentrate on the job any more.	1. I'll be holding our home together.
2. When a man's fighting with his wife all the time, it's certainly not a favorable atmosphere for the children.	2. There'll be a big hassle over who's going to have the children, and I want to be with them day in and day out while they're growing up.
	3. I'd be a lot better off financially.

After studying these balance sheets, Louis decided to try to work things out with Jean.

"A lot of our battling has been over little things," he told me. "We've both got to try to grow up, that's all. At least it's worth another trial."

And this makes a lot of sense. For every one of us is actually "on trial" every day of his life, in his home, on the job, or wherever he goes.

And here's how Allan T., who was interested in the field of advertising, set up his balance sheets on the various possible solutions to his problem of getting started in this field.

POSSIBLE SOLUTION NO. 1—SOME KIND OF JOB
WITH A LEADING NEW YORK ADVERTISING AGENCY

DISADVANTAGES	ADVANTAGES
1. About the best job I could get, to start with, would be in the market research depart-	1. Experience in market research is a good background for an advertising copywriter

ment—interviewing consumers and dealers and summarizing the results of market surveys.

2. I'm not sure that the "market research" approach to the field of advertising is the best one for me.

or an agency account executive, and either job ties in with my general interests and abilities.

2. I would be associating with some top people in the advertising business—when in the office.

3. Experience with a big advertising agency is salable background.

4. New York offers the best opportunity for extending my contacts in this field.

POSSIBLE SOLUTION NO. 2—A JOB SELLING ADVERTISING FOR A NEWSPAPER, MAGAZINE, RADIO OR TV STATION

DISADVANTAGES

1. The only selling jobs I could hope to get, to start with, are in the classified advertising department of a New York newspaper or a small local New York radio station.

2. The pressure on a classified advertising salesman or a time salesman for a local radio station to get business, is heavy.

3. The unit of sale is small and you've got to make a lot of sales before they amount to much in dollars.

ADVANTAGES

1. I know I can sell.

2. The classified advertising managers I've met seem to know a lot about selling.

3. I'd be calling on a lot of different kinds and types of accounts, and getting a wide variety of experience and contacts.

4. I'd have a chance to help write simple ads.

5. Selling classified advertising or local radio time is supposed to be good training for the sale of national space or time.

POSSIBLE SOLUTION NO. 3—A JOB IN THE ADVERTISING DEPARTMENT OF A NATIONAL MANUFACTURER

DISADVANTAGES	ADVANTAGES
1. I'd be dealing with only one type of product.	1. National manufacturers seem to offer the most comprehensive training programs for young men graduating from college.
2. Most of the opportunities with national manufacturers are outside New York City.	2. Experience with a big national advertiser carries a lot of prestige—whether a man later lands with an advertiser, an agency, or an advertising medium.
	3. A big national advertiser looks at advertising from all angles—copywriting, copy testing, media selection, merchandising, promotion—and this gives a young man entering the field a good chance to find out what phase of advertising interests him most.

After giving careful study to the relative advantages and disadvantages, as he saw them, of each of these three possible solutions, this young man decided that the best possible solution for him would be a job in the advertising department of a national manufacturer—at least to start with.

✪ It All Depends On Your Facts and Your Judgment

Now that you have seen exactly what is involved in the four steps in straight thinking—and the extent to which facts and human judgments are involved in the process—you will readily understand that we cannot always be 100 percent right in our solutions to ALL our

problems. But we CAN BOOST OUR BATTING AVER-
AGE on sound decisions if we follow the orderly thought
process.

No matter how important a problem is, we can never
get ALL the facts we would like to have. But we can
always get SOME of them. And we can certainly *use
what we already know.*

The main trouble with our everyday thinking is that
we jump to quick conclusions on important problems
when we are tense, tired, hungry, or in a hurry. Then,
AFTER we make a big mistake, we think of facts that
would have saved us from the mistake—facts WE
KNEW ALL THE TIME!

Another thing, when it comes to weighing the evidence on a balance sheet, it is possible to have one
major point in favor of a decision that overbalances a
dozen minor points that may be against it. It is difficult
for anyone to tell you the relative importance of the
various points that might come up in your consideration of a personal problem, for balancing positive evidence against negative evidence is largely a matter of
your own personal judgment.

Briefly, then, the four steps in straight thinking cannot give anyone a brain. But they can show him how to
make the best possible use of the brain he's got.

And certainly, the more *practice* you get at arriving
at judgments, the more you will be able to *improve*
your judgments.

☼ So Practice Thinking This Way

Right now you are in much the same position as the
person who wants to improve his golf game and who has
been told the rules of the game. In spite of his knowledge of these rules, he may step up to the first tee, take
a healthy swing at the ball in the old way, get the same

old slice, and then say, "Gee! I forgot to hold that left arm straight and follow through."

So, he gets up on the tee again and begins to *practice what he knows*. And if he practices enough, the correct swing will become part of his muscular habit motives.

Similarly, the first time you try to apply the four steps in straight thinking to an important problem, you may find that your decision has already been made before you realize it: that you have jumped from a superficial observation to a conclusion instead of proceeding one step at a time.

What you should do when you find that you have jumped to a conclusion without following the four main steps is obviously to start over and proceed in the organized way. And if you keep on doing this, time after time, before long you will have formed the mental habit of using the DELAYED RESPONSE on every important problem and of following the four main steps in straight thinking. Sooner than you expect, this orderly process will tend to become part of your thinking —automatically.

SUMMARIZING THIS CHAPTER
IF YOU'RE INTERESTED IN THINKING STRAIGHT

✔ 1. Learn how to separate what's important from what isn't.

✔ 2. If the problem is UNimportant, make a quick decision with the assurance that it doesn't make much difference which way you decide.

✔ 3. If the problem is important, use the DELAYED RESPONSE, so that you have TIME TO THINK, and then use that time to:

    a. Separate fact from opinion and analyze the facts from the standpoint of WHO, WHAT, WHEN, and WHERE.

    b. Define your REAL problem and consider possible solutions.

    c. Secure evidence on possible solutions.

    d. Weigh the evidence and arrive at a sound conclusion.

✔ 4. PRACTICE these four steps in dealing with every IMPORTANT PROBLEM you face from now on.

10 HOW TO GET ALONG BETTER WITH PEOPLE

No ONE IS SO SELF-SUFFICIENT THAT HE CAN GET what he wants out of life without the help of a great many people—beginning with his mother and ending with his last friend.

No matter what you're after—money, love, ego food, or health—you need people. And it's easier for you to get what you want when people open their minds to you, give you their confidence, and believe in you.

In fact, if everyone you knew, everyone you met, simply believed everything you said, you could have just about anything you want.

The whole trouble is that so many people's minds are closed so much of the time to the things you suggest.

You may not have thought of it in just this way, but

right now you are on one of four mental levels[1] with every person you know: and I mean *everyone,* including the people you live with or work with or associate with socially or in any way at all.

MENTAL LEVEL NO. 1— CLOSED MIND

This is the "doghouse" level in which people think "To hell with you" or "Oh yeah?" No matter what you say, they're "agin'" it. Their minds are closed to anything you suggest.

MENTAL LEVEL NO. 2— OPEN MIND

This is the "show me" level in which people say, "What makes you think so?" These people will *listen* to what you have to say, but you've got to give them plenty of evidence, you've got to prove your point forty ways to Sunday before they'll do what you say.

MENTAL LEVEL NO. 3— CONFIDENCE

These people have confidence in you. Their attitude toward you is cooperative and friendly. They are will-

[1] William J. Reilly, *Successful Human Relations, Principles and Practice in Business, in the Home, and in Government.* New York: Harper & Brothers, 1952.

ing to do what you want, but they want to know the main reasons why, and these reasons have to "make sense."

MENTAL LEVEL NO. 4—
BELIEF

This is the "anything you say is okay by me" level. These people do what you ask without question. They need no evidence, no proof. They *believe* in you.

☼ Find Out Where You Stand

No matter what kind of situation you face with anyone, it's important for you to know exactly what level you are on with the person involved. For this has a lot to do with what you should say to, and how you should act toward, that person.

Now fortunately, you don't have to be a great psychologist to find out exactly where you stand with anyone. All you have to do is to *listen* to what the other person says.

For example, suppose Henry, an overworked husband, arrives home at two o'clock in the morning after a long hard day and night at the office. His wife expected him home for dinner. He tried to 'phone her but the line was always busy, so he never did get in touch with her.

Now here is a situation in which Harry has an excellent opportunity to find out exactly where he stands with his wife.

Suppose Henry closes the front door quietly. This opens his wife's other eye. She calls downstairs, "Is that you, Henry?"

"Yes, dear," he replies wearily.

"Where have you been?" she asks. (She's at his side now, roping her negligee.)

"Working late at the office, dear."

"Well, I was worried about you. I expected you home for dinner. You must be tired, darling," coos the little wife sympathetically. "Don't you want something to eat before you go to bed?"

Now, THERE'S a BELIEF relationship!

Suppose, however, the conversation runs like this:

Henry enters the front door. His wife calls downstairs, "Is that you, Henry?"

"Yes, dear," he replies wearily.

"Where have you been?"

"Working late at the office, dear," he explains.

"Working at the office until *this* time of night?" (she's at his side now, roping her negligee, a puzzled look in her eyes.) "Why—you were supposed to be home for dinner—*remember?* Must have been a mighty important job!"

"It *was*, dear," says Henry. "There was a wire came in from the Chicago office insisting that we finish our reports before tomorrow."

"Well, they've got a nerve! I think they're working you too hard at that old office, darling. They ought to be paying you more money," comments the little wife. "Do you want something to eat before you go to bed?"

Now THERE'S a CONFIDENCE relationship! HIGH confidence!

Suppose, however, the conversation runs something like this:

Enter Henry. His wife calls downstairs, "Is that you, Henry?"

"Yes, dear," he replies wearily.

"Where have YOU been?"

"Working late at the office, dear."

She's at his side now, roping her negligee. But there's a penetrating look about her narrowed eyes.

"Working at the office until *this time of night?*" she asks suspiciously. "Must have been a mighty important job!"

"It was, dear," says Henry. "There was a wire came in from the Chicago office, insisting that we finish our reports before tomorrow."

"Let me see the wire," she demands, holding out her hand.

Henry reaches into his pocket and hands it to her.

She examines it very carefully and then snaps, "What day is this?"

Henry rubs his head, tired and bewildered. "What *day?* Why . . . it's . . . Wednesday, well, it's early Thursday morning."

"Well, I've got news for you. This wire's got last Saturday's date on it! How do you explain that?"

Henry reaches for the wire. "Yes, it has . . . It HAS? Hmm. Well, I'll be damned, it *has!* Now let's see . . . Oh! Can you imagine that? This was a night letter out of Chicago last Saturday night. The boss must have got this by Monday. But you know how he is. He lets things sit on his desk till the last minute. Believe it or not, I didn't get this until today! That kind of burns me up!"

"Yeah! Burns *me* up, too!" she says, and then wants to know: "Was there anybody else working with you tonight?"

"Yeah! Jack was helping me!" is Henry's prompt reply.

"Well, this is all very interesting. It so happens that Jack and Lucy are coming over here to play cards tomorrow night. I'll get Jack's story then. Don't you want something to eat before you go to bed?"

Now, here's a wife who's just OPEN-MINDED, that's all. She'll listen, but she needs an awful lot of evidence.

Suppose, however, the conversation runs something like this:

Henry's here again. His wife calls downstairs.

"Is that you, Henry?"

"Yes, dear."

"Where have you been, you rat? Don't you lie to me!" she snarls. And among other things, she says, "why . . . you *dog!* I'll find out where you *really* were tonight if it's the last thing I do!"

Now *there's* a CLOSED MIND. She's thinking *negatively* in relation to Henry.

You see how easy it is to find out exactly where you stand with anyone?

When you ask your boss for a raise and the boss says, "I've had that in mind for some time: I'll arrange a 10 percent increase beginning next week," you can put your boss on Mental Level No. 4—Belief. But if the boss says "You ought to be thankful you've got a job," check Mental Level No. 1—Closed Mind.

When a mother counsels her daughter against going on the all-night beach party after the junior prom, and her daughter says: "Well, I'd like to go, but I see what you mean. Okay, Mom"—check Mental Level No. 4.

When the housewife slams the door in the salesman's face or hangs up on the telephone solicitor, check Mental Level No. 1.

✡ *Working on a Closed Mind*

Now obviously, it's the closed-minded people who give us most trouble. And since adults are inclined to cover up their inner thoughts, while children are more likely to come right out and say what they think, let's begin with a child's case so that we can see, in clearer relief, how the human mind works and what we are up against when we try to open a closed mind.

Some time ago, at our house, we had vegetable soup for dinner—home-made vegetable soup.

My wife made it, and every member of the family had something nice to say about it. . . . "Delicious!" . . . "Best I've ever tasted!" . . . "What flavor!" . . . Everyone, that is, but our young son, then seven, who sat on my left.

He just sat there—wouldn't touch it.

I could see that the next course was going to be served pretty soon so I gave him the elbow and nodded toward his soup so he would get started.

He looked up and gave me the "No" sign.

"Come on, you're getting behind," I told him. "Eat your soup."

"I don't like vegetable soup," he replied.

Now I was born and raised in a middle-class Irish family up over the hills from the blast furnaces of Pittsburgh, and I was taught to eat what was put in front of me and be glad to get it. And here was this stubborn kid of ours turning down a good healthful food like home-made vegetable soup.

So I certainly believed that I was right in feeling that this boy, like the rest of our children, should learn to eat what's put in front of him.

I'm *right* about this—RIGHT?

So I proceeded to tell him so in no uncertain terms—which was my first mistake, for he still didn't touch his soup.

Paste this in your hat. *Never take the position, "I'm right about this," if you want to open a closed mind.*

I tried another approach. I tried logic. I thought of

an absolutely air-tight reason for getting him at least to *try* the soup—a reason that you can't get around logically.

"How can you say that you don't like *this* vegetable soup when you haven't even tasted it?" I argued.

But this kid got around it. "I don't like *any* vegetable soup," was his pat reply.

And this was my second mistake. So hear this.

Never use logic on a human being with a closed mind.

By this time I was getting a little hot under the collar.

"Look, if you don't know how to eat with the rest of the family, if you're going to make the whole dinner unpleasant, take that dish of vegetable soup into the playroom and don't leave the playroom until it's finished," I commanded.

Which brings up my third mistake and the third thing to paste in your hat whenever you're trying to open a closed mind.

Never take a flat-footed position from which you cannot retreat.

The boy marched off to the playroom with his vegetable soup, spilling a little on the way. Soon we had all finished our soup and the main course was served.

Things began to quiet down around the dinner table. Everybody began to look at *me* as if *I* had done something, instead of the kid!

I know when I'm licked.

With no report from the playroom, I got up from the table, walked out of the dining room, down the hall, and into the playroom and there sat my son.

The soup hadn't been touched.

Here was a young man whose mind *and mouth* were both closed to vegetable soup.

And before I had a chance to open my mouth, he up

and said, "You know, Daddy, you can't *force* someone to like vegetable soup. That's not straight thinking."

That was enough for me.

Even though I still felt that I was right and he was wrong, it was apparent that up to this point I was getting nowhere in my efforts to open his mind to vegetable soup. So I reversed my field completely.

"Okay!" I said. "You're right about that. I lost my head. I made a mistake. Leave it there. Come on in and eat the rest of your dinner."

And he did.

Later that evening, when I took him upstairs and sat on the side of his bed and kissed him good night and told him I loved him, he put his hand over on my arm and said, reassuringly, "Daddy . . . you don't have to worry about making that mistake at dinner."

"WHO? ME? . . . Oh . . . Well, all right. I lost my head. I made a mistake. But there must be *some* way to get you to like vegetable soup. And I want you to help me find that way. If YOU ever get any ideas on the subject, let me know."

Suddenly the boy offered a solution.

"I know how to get me to like vegetable soup," he said, softly.

"You DO?" I gasped. "Well, come on, GIVE!"

"Just don't have it again for a long long time," he counseled. "Then I'll get to like it. That's how I got to like spinach."

"Yeah . . . that figures," I told him.

"Another thing, Daddy," he continued, "you're married."

"Well, I *hope* so, with all you kids running around the house. But what's that got to do with it?"

"Well—you *never* have to eat what *you* don't like. All

you have to do is tell Mommy what you want for dinner and you get it. What do I have to do—wait till I get married before I get what I like?"

"No, boy. You don't have to wait till you get married," I assured him. "Keep your shirt on."

Then, for the first time, I began to see a little patch of blue in my mind and an idea began to shine through.

"What do you want for dinner tomorrow night?" I asked him.

He sat up on one elbow. *Now* he was interested. Now his mind *was* open—wide open.

Cube steak, string beans, mashed potatoes, and ice cream with chocolate sauce and nuts was his selection.

"Okay . . . that's what we'll have. Come to think of it, this will help Mommy to solve one of the greatest problems she has because she's always wondering what to have for dinner that people will like. But if we eat what you like tomorrow night, will you eat what Ann likes on Tuesday night, and what Myrt likes on Wednesday night, and what Mommy likes on Thursday night? And I work here. I get a night, too. Right?"

"Oh, sure," the boy agreed whole-heartedly. "And then it'll be *my* turn again."

"Oh, sure." And we had a man-to-man handshake right then and there.

About two months later, when it was my night to select what we would eat for dinner, I got the idea from some place or other that we ought to have vegetable soup. It just came to me.

And, believe it or not, when vegetable soup was served that night, the boy ate it.

So it's apparent to me, and I know by this time it must be to you, that it often takes a lot of *time* and a lot of *thought* and a lot of *patience* to open a closed mind.

True, I could have *forced* my son to eat his soup in

the first place. But he wouldn't have liked it. And, more important to me, he wouldn't have liked *me*.

When you come right down to it, in most of our everyday relations with grownups, we certainly can't *force* them to do anything—even if we're right and they're wrong.

We must rely on *persuasion*.

And you haven't a ghost of a chance when you try to use the logic of persuasion on a closed mind.

You must first open it.

☼ The One Sure Way To Open a Closed Mind

Now if we review exactly what happened in the battle with my son, we find that I got nowhere as long as I opposed him. For after all, *opposition closes the mind*. But the moment I began to *agree with him* and *help him to be right*, his mind began to open.

"Yes . . . but wait a minute," you say. "You're not going to ask me to agree with a person and help him to be right when I know he's wrong and I'm right, are you?"

Well, you're absolutely right when you say that agreeing with people and helping them to be right won't get you anywhere—if you stop there.

That's merely the first step.

Bear in mind that when you're dealing with a person whose mind is closed, your first job is to open it. And it's always possible to find at least one or two points you can agree on with the other fellow if you make a deliberate effort to look for these points.

No matter how right you think you are, there's a pretty good chance that the other fellow is not a total moron, and if you invite him to spell out his position so that you will fully understand it, he may have something to say which would influence you.

Then, if you go one step further and make an active effort to put yourself in the other person's place and to help him to be right, what you are actually doing is opening *your own mind* to his point of view.

When you do this and are perfectly sincere about it, the other person is much more likely to open *his* mind to listen to *your side of the question.*

In the process, you may learn something that will change your thinking and the other fellow may, too.

I'll admit it's not easy. But if you are mentally able to transplant yourself into the other person's mind and assume his point of view, you have a good chance of rounding out a complete picture of the facts and of finding out and admitting if the other fellow's partly right and you're wrong in some respects. And once you prove yourself capable of doing this, the other fellow is inclined to want to prove that he is capable of being just as fair and just as open-minded as you are—with the result that he will see and admit points where you are right and he's wrong.

As you know, whenever any two people open their minds to each other, they are well on the way toward a common agreement. On the other hand, two closed-minded people may argue forever and not arrive anywhere.

✡ Some Practical Applications

Now let's see how this works out in actual practice.

Let's take a case that's about as tough as you can get—politics.

Not long ago at luncheon two good friends of mine, let's call them Adams and Brown, Democrat and Republican (or Brown and Adams, Republican and Democrat, whichever party order you prefer), got into a real first-class political hassle. They were getting just about as far as arguments between two political partisans ever get. In fact, it began to look to me as if they were building up a beautiful enmity. They certainly weren't building a beautiful friendship and neither one was getting anywhere with the other.

Then an interesting thing happened.

One of them (and I'm not saying who because I'm staying out of this) reached over, put his hand on his opponent's arm, and said, "Look, Fred . . . I'm perfectly willing to admit that your party has produced a lot of great men." And then he went on to name five or six of them.

That did it. He had introduced an area of agreement. And before you could say Jack Robinson, Fred began to reel off the names of great men in the other fellow's political party.

And the upshot of the whole thing was that before the luncheon was over, they both agreed that while each had a favorite political party, America is fortunate to have the two-party system and that when it came to a showdown, neither one of them would blindly vote for a bad candidate in either political party.

Now I don't know whether either one of these gentlemen will ever cross party lines and vote for the other's candidate, but they both certainly were more *open-minded* at the end of this discussion than they were in the beginning. And this is *Step One* toward looking at the facts about both candidates in any election.

Nearly everyone seems to be interested in getting a raise nowadays, and here is a case that is typical of hundreds of instances I've observed first-hand in counseling men and women on their career problems.

An assistant office manager for a New York toiletries manufacturer had been after his boss for a raise for some time; but he got nowhere for the simple reason that his boss felt that Joe was getting paid all he was worth, whereas Joe complained to me that his boss was a tightwad.

I told Joe to reverse his attitude toward his boss and to start helping his boss to be right, and to begin by trying to figure out how he could make himself more valuable to the company.

So Joe had a talk with his boss and explained that he would like to *earn* a raise by making himself more useful and that he would appreciate it if his boss would give him any extra assignments that would help him to do this.

Meanwhile, Joe himself began thinking more about his job and how he could improve on what he was doing.

First of all, he came up with the idea that the company might save a lot of valuable downtown New York office space by storing inactive records in the Hoboken warehouse.

Then, before Joe went on his vacation, he worked up a little job instruction folder for the man who took his place. This proved so helpful that the boss adopted the very same pattern for writing up every job in the office so that it would be easier for someone to take over when a person is away for any reason. And these standard work instructions for each job help a lot in training new employees, too.

By this time Joe was a different person. He never complained now about his boss, and all he talked about was the new improvements he was working on.

And I wasn't one bit surprised when Joe was recently promoted to office manager with a nice increase in salary.

Now, what Joe did wasn't so difficult. Any person can *earn* a raise and a promotion simply by looking at things from the boss's point of view and figuring out better ways of doing things.

✿ Removing the Pressure

One of the most successful magazine space salesmen I know told me that he had called on a prospect for years and was absolutely convinced that the prospect should buy.

But he never did.

The prospect contended that he was perfectly satisfied with the magazines he was using, that he had tested them out through the years, and that he saw no sense in taking a chance on any new ones.

The salesman had worn himself out trying to prove, with facts and figures, that he was right and the prospect was wrong.

One day the salesman got so weary that he changed his tactics.

"I'm convinced," he told the prospect, "that you ought to be using my magazine. But apparently you're right and I'm wrong. You see, I'm on a tough spot. My boss expects me to sell you. I'd almost be willing to pay for a test ad myself, just to see whether it pays out. Maybe I've been wrong in trying to sell you my magazine at all if those other magazines you're using pay out so much better."

As soon as the salesman stopped trying to prove the prospect was wrong, the pressure was off.

"Well," said the prospect, "I guess neither one of us can really be sure until we test it. Okay, we'll try a small test ad."

The test ad paid out and the prospect turned into a regular customer.

Any good salesman will tell you that even if he's 100 percent right and the prospect is 100 percent wrong, this isn't enough to assure him of an order. "Winning an argument and losing a sale" is so common that any salesman worthy of the name will readily agree that "thinking with the prospect" and "helping him to be right" is the first step toward more sales and more profits.

And this is a good lesson for anyone to learn, for we're all trying to sell something.

As Charles M. Schwab, master of human relations, said: "Many of us think of salesmen as people traveling around with sample kits. Instead, we are all salesmen every day of our lives. We are selling our ideas, our plans, our energies, our enthusiasm to those with whom we come in contact."

And any time we are in so much of a hurry to get what we want that we permit ourselves to get into a big fat argument with a closed mind, instead of taking the time and exercising the patience required to open that mind, we are violating one of the simplest laws of human behavior and we might as well be running backwards.

☆ Help the Other Fellow To Be Right

We are not nearly so likely to violate the laws of our physical environment—for a very good reason. If you are on the second floor of your home or the tenth floor of an office building, no matter how much of a hurry you are in to get downstairs, you wouldn't *think* of jumping out the window. Why . . . it might upset your whole morning! The penalty for violating the law of gravity is *immediate!*

But we often violate laws of human behavior, without seeming to suffer any penalty at all, because there is usually a *delayed reaction* involved. We may offend a person without suffering any obvious penalty for years. We are actually unaware of many of the mistakes we make. And because we are so ingenious in rationalizing the mistakes we *are* aware of—satisfying ourselves that *we* are right and the other fellow is wrong—we are able to go to sleep at night with the general satisfaction that other people may be stupid or crazy but *we're* all right.

It doesn't take much brains to figure out why a person opens his mind to you when you agree with him and help him to be right. The simplest possible explanation of this is that one of the deepest desires in the human heart is to prove that we are right.

Everyone wants to be "right." We can't sleep at night until we've satisfied ourselves that we are right, no matter what we did during the day.

Until we do, our subconscious mind keeps banging away at us and we can't get any rest. It's what psychologists have for years been calling "rationalization."

Even a fellow who commits murder can't eat or sleep until he has satisfied himself that he was justified.

So isn't it clear that when you help someone to be right, you are satisfying one of his greatest desires—one of his greatest needs?

No wonder he opens his mind to you!

Think of the people you know. Isn't it true that you open your mind to those who agree with you and think you are right about things? And isn't it equally true that you close your mind to those who oppose you and find fault with you?

Take your present situation right now. Are you having trouble with your wife or your husband or your boss or your children or with anyone else?

If so, just look into the mirror and ask yourself, "What did I do wrong *this* time?" Then go to that

person and admit that you made some kind of mistake
—and you'll open his or her mind and be well on your
way to eliminating the trouble.

After all, you *did* make some kind of mistake in dealing with that person or you wouldn't be in trouble. Yes,
I know—the other person may have made a mistake,
too. But *if* you are *big* enough to admit your mistake
first, he will be far more willing to admit his mistake.

You may not believe this. Then you never will believe
it until you try it.

I never believed it myself until I tried it.

The whole trouble is that we all masquerade too
much. We are inclined to put on the false whiskers and
try to act like Superman. But we can never enjoy the
admiration and respect and affection of others by trying to act perfect. For after all, no one can ever succeed
in appearing perfect or be happy in trying to.

We all want to be loved and respected for what we
really are—well-meaning but *im*perfect.

We would all like to quit the false and futile attitude
of trying to appear infallible. We're willing to admit
that we make mistakes if others would only do the same.

Trouble is, we expect the other fellow to admit his
mistakes FIRST.

If you will only take the initiative and stop trying to
act as if you were always right, others will usually
admit their weaknesses, too.

It's all as simple as that.

"I was wrong."

"I made a mistake."

Tough words to say. But they do open the other fellow's mind.

Your ability to open a person's mind, then, depends
entirely on your mental attitude toward that person

and your mental attitude toward yourself—your willingness to open your *own* mind to your *own* mistake and your willingness to understand the other person and to help him to be right. And opening his mind is your FIRST STEP toward getting him to believe what you say and do what you want.

As we shall see, there's a right time and a wrong time to use logic and facts and figures. There's no use trying to use proof material on a mind that's closed. You've got to open it first.

☆ How To EARN a Person's Confidence

On a New York cross-town bus I saw a little boy, about five years old, point to the library building at Forty-second Street and Fifth Avenue, and ask his father, who was reading a newspaper:

"Is that your office, Daddy?"

"No, that's a library."

"What's in a library?" asked the boy.

"Books."

"What does it say in those books?"

"It says to mind your Daddy. Now shut up."

You know the kind of questions children ask.

"Is that the biggest ship in the world, Daddy?"

"Mommy, where's that airplane going?"

"When's *our* dog going to have babies?"

These are serious questions to a child, and any parent who habitually brushes them off with careless answers, is on the way to losing the *confidence* of his child. For when the child gets a little older, and finds that his parents were so often wrong, you can hardly expect him to accept with complete confidence other statements, however wise, that they may make.

It's only reasonable to expect that any fair-minded

child, after learning that his parents' answers don't square with the teacher's, will soon think to himself, "Gee, the old folks must be slipping."

One morning an insurance salesman called me over the 'phone from the reception room.

"I'm not going to try to sell you any insurance. All I want is ten minutes of your time to explain a brand new policy that our company developed especially for men like you."

I opened my mind to this fellow, but when he got into my office, he *did* try to sell me some insurance, he *didn't* leave in ten minutes, and the brand new policy that his company offered *wasn't* developed especially for a man like me.

Obviously, we can't earn anyone's confidence with careless statements that we don't even believe ourselves.

There's nothing mysterious about earning a person's confidence. It depends on our everyday thoughts and actions in little things as well as in big things.

Day in and day out, in casual relations and vital relations with others, we are continually in the process of either GAINING or LOSING the confidence of those who open their minds to us.

Their estimate of us either rises or falls, depending on what we say and what we do.

Hundreds of instances, some of major, some of minor, importance, race through my mind: instances that include the extravagant claims made by a job applicant trying to impress a prospective employer, tl.e woman who had too many drinks at the Christmas party, the salesman who padded his expense account, the mother who broke her promise, the clerk who told me that the shirt wouldn't shrink.

But whenever you feed an open-minded person with *favorable* evidence, *you earn his confidence*. And anyone is favorably impressed when you show him that you are thinking and acting in terms of *his* interests as well as your own.

)⸏⸏(

FIVE SIMPLE RULES
FOR WINNING CONFIDENCE

▪⸏⸏

In fact, this is the first of five simple rules to bear in mind in attempting to earn the confidence of any open-minded person.

✡ Rule 1. Think of the Other Person's Interests

Sure, it's obvious, but let's face the obvious. Man is primarily interested in himself. That's the way man is made. That's the way you are. That's the way I am. As Josh Billings said, "Most men are like eggs. Too full of themselves to hold anything else."

And Maxwell Droke writes:[1]

> Let's begin by asking, "What interests you?"
> And the answer is—You.
> Yes, you are by far the most fascinating person in all the world—*to yourself*. This sounds selfish and egotistical. It is. But it is also human. It is perfectly natural and normal that your primary interest should be in yourself—your hopes, fears, ambitions, triumphs. The whole universe centers around you and your own little family circle. This is so obvious a truism that it should require no emphasis.

So, if you want to gain the confidence of this "full-of-himself" person, you've got to tell him what *he's* going to get out of doing what you suggest. *And this promise of yours had better come true!*

---

[1] Maxwell Droke, *People—How to Get Them To Do What You Want Them To Do*. Indianapolis: privately printed, 1939.

It's easy for you to "put one over" on an open mind—
once. And unless you spend your time thinking in
terms of the other fellow's interests, as well as of your
own, you may find yourself inadvertently taking advantage of him. Whenever this happens, it's just too bad
for you.

It's easy for a salesman to yield to the temptation of
recommending the "buy" that gives him the largest
commission; but if that sale turns out to the disadvan-
tage of the buyer, he's lost a good customer.

A salesman, or anyone else, can study the tricks of the
trade and acquire a pleasing personality that opens
people's minds and persuades them to act, but if the
person who acts later regrets his action, the salesman,
or anyone else, has an enemy on his hands instead of a
friend.

Even though he may not recognize it, a butcher, a
baker, a politician, a salesman, a lawyer, or anyone else,
may be more interested in what he gets than in what he
gives, and when others see evidence of this, they lose
confidence.

But if you can overcome this human tendency we all
have, of thinking primarily in terms of your own immediate selfish interests; if you can sell yourself on the
proposition that in the long run your own self-interests
are best served by fully protecting the interests of others
as well, your heart is more likely to be in the right place
and it is easier for you to say and do the things that
earn the lasting confidence of others.

Open-minded people actually *want* to have confidence in you. They don't want to go to the endless
trouble of checking and double-checking everything
you say.

Life is altogether too complex to permit us to check
up on every possible angle before we act. People are

hired, goods and services are bought, directions are followed, fortunes change hands, lives are pledged, simply because people have confidence in others.

☆ Rule 2. Select the Right Time To Present Your Ideas

Anyone who has ever swung a baseball bat, a golf club, or a tennis racket, knows the *importance of proper timing*. He knows that poor timing makes the ball fly in the wrong direction. And anyone who plays cards knows that there's a right time and a wrong time to play an Ace.

Yet in our business and personal life the importance of timing is often forgotten.

No matter what you're trying to get anyone to do, there is a right time and a wrong time to present your ideas on the subject. Everyone has his "moments," and it's up to you to be patient and bide your time until those moments come.

People give you clear and unmistakable signals that tell you when to present your evidence and when not to.

Some time ago some friends of ours asked me if I would talk to their young son about his habit of building fires in the cellar. And one afternoon at their home I was all primed to get into conversation with this flaming youth—waiting my chance to open up the subject.

I had no more than opened my mouth to speak when he beat me to the conversational punch with "d'ya know any wisecracks?"

I was quick to sense that what I had planned to say to this child would have been improperly timed. So I dusted off a few wisecracks. In fact, we spent all the allotted time with wisecracks—I picking up a few new ones—and we never did get down to hot cellars.

But he did ask me to come back. So at least his mind

is *open* to me. Perhaps I'll get another chance at him soon . . . if he doesn't burn the house down in the meantime.

As a rule, you don't get anywhere with others when either you or they are at a white heat. And yet that's the very time when many family problems are likely to get an airing.

The father whose daughter had been staying out late and who decided to "wait up for her *this* time and settle this thing once and for all"; the parents who read the riot act to their two children when guests were present; the wife who proceeded to explain the game of bridge to her recalcitrant husband while the other players sat by embarrassed—all these people are guilty of grievous mistakes in timing.

Recently I observed a salesman make a mistake in timing that cost his company plenty. Sitting in the office of a big buyer in Los Angeles, I listened while this salesman began to rush through a lengthy presentation at 2:45 P.M., in spite of the fact that the buyer had explained at the very outset that he had an important meeting at three o'clock.

But the salesman tried to jam things through rather than arrange another appointment. When he asked for the order at about five minutes to three, the buyer turned him down cold. After the salesman had left, the buyer was pretty mad.

"He'll cool his heels a long time before I see him again," he told me.

Anyone can improve his timing and promote better relations with his family, his friends, and his business associates, if he will simply remember that most people are easier to convince when they are fresh, relaxed, properly fed, and at leisure, rather than when they are tense, tired, hungry, or in a hurry.

If you're talking to a hungry man, don't try to convince him of anything until after you have fed him. If you're talking to someone who is tired, you'd better wait until he's rested. If you're talking to someone who's in a huff about something, you'd better wait until he cools off. If you want someone to do you a favor, don't try to jump into his lap while he's running for a train.

This matter of timing is important in all kinds of human situations. It's so easy to say the right thing at the wrong time. But after all, people do give you clear signs that tell you when to STOP and when to GO.

If you begin today to wait for the green light before you try to convince anybody of anything, you're bound to increase your chances of getting what you're after.

☼ *Rule 3. Give the Other Person a Reasonably Complete Story*

One of the main reasons for selecting the right time to present your ideas on any subject to anyone else, is that you want to be sure to have sufficient time to present a reasonably complete statement of your case.

A little information is a dangerous thing. It may even be misleading. And we cannot hope to gain the confidence of an open mind unless we fully inform that mind.

Yet in our homes, in our business, and in our social relations, we often fail to give sufficient thought to the preparation of our case.

Husbands and wives are always in danger of making some sudden proposal to buy this or that, or go here or there, without spelling things out sufficiently to each other. A husband will call up his wife at five o'clock and tell her that he's bringing a business associate home for dinner—without apologizing for the sudden move and without explaining that this will help him to close a sale. And a wife will suddenly tell her husband that she has to have a new stove or new slipcovers or a new coat right away—without going into the reasons soon enough to avoid an argument.

Employees by the thousands drop ideas into company suggestion boxes thereby hoping to get favorable recognition, but a surprisingly small number of these ideas are well thought out and fully developed.

Some employers are making the belated discovery that it is up to them to keep their workers reasonably well informed about the various factors that influence their business, if they are to gain and to hold the confidence of their employees. Simple, easy-to-read, easy-to-understand annual reports are just as interesting to the workers as they are to the stockholders. An explanation of the outside factors that may affect the business in the days to come—factors over which the company has no control—helps the worker to understand the true reasons for changes in wage rates, temporary layoffs, or any other conditions of employment that are of vital interest to him.

Many salesmen fail because they never get over their complete story, which is the only sound basis for gaining the prospect's confidence and asking for the order.

I asked a brilliant attorney, "How do you explain the fact that you win such a high percentage of your cases?"

"It's because my opponents are too lazy to prepare their cases," he replied.

☆ Rule 4. Keep It Brief, Make It Interesting

In giving the other person a reasonably complete story, be sure that you don't *bore* the listener. Be brief. And make it interesting.

The importance of the case dictates the length of your presentation. Obviously, you shouldn't take more than a few minutes to effect a minor sale or ask a minor favor. And even if you're trying to put over a deal that involves millions of dollars, or to propose something that affects the lives of thousands of people, you'd better not count on sustained attention for more than an hour at a time.

You know how impatient *you* get when someone rambles on and on endlessly and insists on boring you with a lot of *unrelated detail* that does not interest you in the least.

When Mrs. Broody calls up Mrs. Brady and asks her to take a table at the bridge benefit for the local hospital, Mrs. Brady may be interested if she is told who is going to attend, what they are going to have to eat, and what the prizes are. But she may suddenly take a dim view of the whole thing if she has to listen to a lot of cute reports on Mrs. Broody's grandchildren.

Not long ago I attended a conference in which a brilliant young inventor explained his latest brain child to some financiers. Their minds were open. They had asked for the meeting. It was an important meeting for this young inventor. It was his big chance. The men he was talking to had the money and the connections to put his invention over.

We arrived at the inventor's workshop shortly before noon and were seated in front of a huge blackboard covered with technical charts and graphs.

The inventor began talking at twelve o'clock sharp and two hours later he was still talking about all the troubles he had to go through to develop his big idea.

At ten minutes after two, one of the financiers exploded.

"Look!" he interrupted the inventor. "We've been listening to you for over two hours. You've led us into the jungle of your scientific adventures, pointing out

every difficulty—every single dark cave you've got yourself into—and you've explained in detail how you finally
fought your way out. And we're still not out of the
woods! I *still* don't know what you've got or what it'll
do for me!"

"I'm coming to that," assured the inventor. "But you
men don't know what I've been through . . ."

"Look," the financier interrupted again. "People are
not interested in processes. People are interested in
results. People will never know what 'you've been
through!' People don't care! That's the secret cross
you'll have to bear alone. People don't give a hoot how
difficult it was for you to arrive at something worthwhile.
They want to know what it will do for *them*."

Believe me, my sympathies were with the inventor
but I couldn't help feeling that old Mr. Moneybags was
right.

☆ Rule 5. Watch Your Promises

In periods of anxiety or when we're trying to make a
big impression on someone, it is easy to let our enthusiasm run away with us and to make promises that are
not easy to fulfill.

A father was so anxious to get his son, who was a
freshman in college, to study harder and to improve his
marks, that he promised to let his son go to Europe for
the summer if he finished the school year with a "C"
average. They boy got the "C" average, but the father
didn't have the money to send his son to Europe.

A sales manager who was falling behind on quotas,
promised his boss that "we'll wind up the year with an
increase." But when the end of the year came, the increase wasn't there.

It's always a big temptation to win a quick victory

with a big promise. But when the evidence catches up with you, you pay a heavy price in lost confidence.

All of us make careless promises that we don't have to make at all. We don't have to "promise the moon" in order to get a person to act favorably. In fact, we are more likely to lose a person's confidence with such promises.

One of the wisest teachers I ever had, Dr. Walter F. Rittman, told me, "Never make an unqualified promise about the future."

Certainly it is vital in all our human relations to see to it that *any promise we do make really comes true.*

HOW TO *DESERVE* A PERSON'S BELIEF

A belief relationship with anyone represents the highest plane of human relations. To believe in one another is not only the most civilized, most satisfying, and most beautiful form of human relationship, it is the most efficient. It saves so much time.

All of us would like to feel that we are worthy of the belief of at least a few people who are nearest and dearest to us. And we are, if we have consistently served these people down through the years.

And there are two main things to bear in mind if you wish to extend your belief relationships to an ever-widening circle of people—as I know you do.

✿ 1. Show Belief Yourself

Belief inspires belief. And you must believe in others if you would have them believe in you.

One of the best tests of this is to put down on paper

the names of those in whom *you* believe. Then put down the names of those who believe in you. You needn't be surprised if you find the same names on both lists.

If you cannot honestly say to yourself that you enjoy such a relationship with at least a few people, you can safely conclude to yourself, privately, that you still have some work to do in developing your own capacity for belief in others.

However, just believing in a person in one kind of situation doesn't mean that you must necessarily believe in him in an entirely different situation.

For example, you may trust a business advisor with practically every dollar you have. But if he asks you to take a ride in his new airplane, your mind may be closed.

Even a wife might believe in her husband as a great provider, but she may feel that he is "a total loss" socially. And a husband may believe in his wife completely in her handling of the children, but he may have very little confidence in her on the golf course.

In other words, the number of people who deserve your *complete* belief in *any* and *every* possible kind of situation, will be relatively few.

Every now and then you have the high privilege of knowing a person who deserves your whole-hearted belief in every possible kind of situation of any importance—a person with good judgment in all kinds of personal, social, and business situations.

In order to build the belief relationships that mean the most to you, with very many people you must make a conscious effort to do so. You must *think* in terms of enjoying belief relationships with as many people as possible or you will never attain such a continuing relationship even among those who are fully deserving.

For example, the businessman who does not believe

that anyone else is capable of performing a job as well as he and who is continually checking and double-checking and hounding the other fellow the moment he gives him a job to do, seldom rises to an executive position. Even if he owns his own business, it will always be a "one-man band."

In the home, the wife who is continually cross-questioning her husband concerning his motives, his work, and where he has been every minute of the time on his night off, gradually destroys any confidence or belief relationship with her husband. And the same goes for the double-checking husband.

On the other hand, those most loved, most respected, and most successful as parents, friends, associates, and leaders, are invariably those who have the capacity for believing in others and showing it.

The greatest prize you can offer anyone is your belief in him. He needs the belief of others to give him *self*-respect. You give a person your belief, your whole-hearted belief, your unqualified belief, your no-strings-attached belief, and that person will rarely let you down. When you believe in a person, it is practically impossible for him to return your trust with meanness or treachery or deceit. For in doing so, he would lose his own self-respect.

☼ 2. Ask the Person To Believe in You

Any time you feel that you have gained a person's confidence and have demonstrated repeatedly that you are worthy of his belief, the time has come for you to ASK that person to believe in you.

I don't mean that you should simply say, "Do you believe in me?" For the other person could say "Yes," and your relationship still wouldn't mean anything until it came to a test.

I mean you should ask the person to believe in you by *testing* your relationship—*by asking him to do something of some importance without giving him any evidence to prove why he should do it.*

For instance, one day at my hotel in Chicago I had a long-distance telephone call from the president of a large organization who had retained me to work on some of their marketing problems. He told me he had to select a man for an important executive position with his company and wanted to know whether I could recommend anyone.

I knew I had this executive's confidence. I had already given him plenty of evidence. Now I wanted to move him into a belief relationship.

So instead of giving him my candidate's name and telling him all the reasons why I felt he should select this man, I merely said: "Your problem is solved. I know the right man for the job."

"What's that?" he asked.

I repeated: "Your problem is solved. I know the right man for the job." Then I added, "Now we're talking long-distance. Is there anything else you want me to do?"

"Why . . . that's wonderful!" he said. Then he talked briefly about another matter, and concluded by saying, "If you're sure you have the right man, go ahead and get him as soon as possible."

If this executive had insisted on having some evidence as to who the man was, I'd have given it to him, and understood that I merely had his confidence. But when he didn't, this proved that *he believed in me.* I found the right man in a branch office of this same organization, recommended him, and he was appointed.

From that instant on, I never accompanied my recommendations to this chief executive with a lot of evidence. And I did what he asked, without question. In fact, whenever he offered "reasons," I would interrupt, saying, "If that's what you want, I'll do it. You don't have to take any of your valuable time explaining *why* to me!"

This approach saved us both a lot of time and expense. And by showing my belief in him, I inspired and preserved his belief in me.

No matter where you go, if you listen to what people say, you will find them seeking the belief of others— and sometimes getting it.

A housewife phones her butcher.

"Can you get me a real nice turkey around twelve pounds?"

"Yes, Mrs. Jones, I'll get you a nice one."

"What kind are you going to get?" she asks.

"Leave it to me, Mrs. Jones. I've never sent you a poor turkey yet, have I?"

"All right," says Mrs. Jones. "I'll depend on you to pick out a nice one as you always do."

Now the butcher asked for her belief by reminding her that he was worthy of it, and he got it.

I sat in an executive's office and heard him say to his wife over the phone, "I know you believe in my judgment in such matters, dear." Then she said something. Then he said, "Well, that's fine. You just leave it entirely in my hands."

After he hung up, he turned to me and said, "You see, that illustrates your idea of asking a person to believe in you when you *deserve* that belief. My wife just called to discuss the purchase of a Christmas present for a relative in California. You heard what I said. She feels quite relieved about the whole matter. This idea of asking the other person to believe in your judgment has saved me a lot of time. I used to have all kinds of long-drawn-out, annoying telephone conversations and discussions, not only with my wife but with people in general."

In every single instance I've given of a person asking someone else to believe in him, you immediately recognized that this was done with the use of a simple ASSURANCE STATEMENT.

"Your problem is solved. I know the right man for the job."

"Leave it to me, Mrs. Jones. I've never sent you a poor turkey yet, have I?"

"Well, that's fine. You just leave it entirely in my hands."

These are just a few of the many ways in which *you* can use an assurance statement and ask people to believe in you. And if you are worthy of their belief, you will get it.

Now after all, the use of assurance statements is quite common. But the main trouble is that people often use assurance statements prematurely.

The time to use an assurance statement comes when you enjoy the confidence of a person and he is ready to believe in you—when you have already *shown* that person that you *deserve* his belief.

✡ What Confidence and Belief Relationships Can Mean to You

Whatever progress you make toward getting what you want out of life, depends largely on those who have confidence or belief in you.

To realize this, all you have to do is to remember how you landed your best job or recall how you first met your most valued and most interesting friends. Think of the most satisfactory experiences you've had, the clubs or associations or fraternal organizations you belong to, the sales you've made, or any other kind of successful relation with others, and you'll find, in nearly every case, that you were *sponsored* by someone who had confidence or belief in you.

Anyone knows that you get further faster in all human relations when you have good friends who are willing to vouch for you and give you the old build-up.

You may have a lot on the ball, but if you have no sponsorship *within* your organization, you won't go very far. And if you have no sponsorship *outside* your own organization, you won't get very many attractive job offers.

If you are a housewife and have no sponsorship in your community, you will find yourself being left out of many interesting clubs and social activities.

As Wilfred Funk said in a recent radio interview with Martha Deane: "If people don't like you, they'll let you go right down the drain. If they do like you, they'll fight for you all the way."

He quoted Charles F. Kettering, famous General Motors scientist, as saying that 90 per cent of success is getting along with people; ten per cent is technique. And then Mr. Funk added, "One of the most important things that everyone should be taught in school is how to get along with people."

It's a wonderful thing to be in tune with those around you. It fills you with a feeling of well-being and deep personal satisfaction.

☼ Getting in Tune with People

In fact, the next time you feel mentally disturbed or upset about anything, just review in your mind what happened to cause this disturbance and you'll probably find that it's all because you're out of harmony with your human environment—you're helping *someone* to be *wrong*.

Then, just turn your mental attitude around and *help that person to be right*. Give him the benefit of every doubt and freely admit to yourself whatever mistakes you even *might* have made.

You'll feel better immediately, and when you see that person again you'll automatically say and do the right things because you feel *right* toward that person. You are in tune with him.

The moment you assume this mental attitude toward others, you find that it is easier for you to get along with others, easier for you to get their cooperation, easier for you to make all your relations with others more satisfying and more productive and more mutually profitable, easier for you to achieve your loftiest desires, easier for you to enjoy more peaceful relations with others at home and abroad.

Yes, help the other fellow to be right and you'll find open minds and open hearts wherever you go.

There is nothing in this world you deserve that you cannot have when people open their minds to you, give you their confidence, and believe in you.

HERE'S WHAT'S IN THIS CHAPTER—FOR YOU TO REMEMBER

✔ 1. To open a closed mind:
  a. *Listen* to what the other person has to say.
  b. Find *some area of agreement* and *help him to be right!*
  c. Never take the position "I'm right about this."
  d. Never use logic on a closed mind.
  e. Never take a flat-footed position from which you cannot retreat.

✔ 2. To earn a person's confidence:
  a. Think of the other person's interests.
  b. Watch your *timing!*
  c. Give the person a reasonably complete story.
  d. Be brief. Make it interesting. Tell him what HE'S going to get out of it.
  e. Watch your promises.

✔ 3. To deserve a person's belief:
  a. Show belief yourself.
  b. *Ask* the person to believe in you.

11

YOUR OWN

PERSONAL DESIGN

FOR ACHIEVEMENT

IF YOU HAVE FOLLOWED THE SUGGESTIONS FOUND IN Part One of this book, you have some rather specific definitions—in writing—of what you want out of life, right now.

And if you have studied the previous chapters in Part Two, you have some definite plans for getting what you want—one step at a time.

However, even after you get started in the right direction and actually begin to make your dreams come true by your own thoughts and your own efforts, it is important to remember that no matter how successful you become or how great your achievements turn out to be, you must always continue to work toward EVEN

GREATER ACCOMPLISHMENTS IN THE FUTURE.

For this is the law of growth.

Any time you begin to get pretty well satisfied with yourself and your vision for the future becomes shorter than your past achievements, you begin to live in the past. You begin to die. Nature begins to kill you. And why shouldn't she?

Let us see, then, how you can keep extending your vision for the future and gradually build your own personal design for achievement.

DESIGNS FOR MEN

☼ *If You're Under Thirty-five*

If you are a normal young man, you are either married or you have some ideas on when you would like to be married and start raising a family. If you are not married and haven't found the right girl yet, you should deliberately set about to do so. There are innumerable church and community activities and there are many courses of study that will put you into contact with the kind of girls you would like to meet. The rest is up to you.

As far as your vocational desires are concerned, your *primary and immediate objective* in your chosen field is to *build a salable background, if possible, before you are thirty-five.*

By a salable background, I mean training in good schools and experience with favorably-known organizations which will help you to sell your services in the future at the right price.

How much money you make before thirty-five is not nearly so important as whether you are gaining such salable education and experience. For the *peak earning years* (unless you're a professional athlete or a movie star) usually come *after* a man passes the thirty-five-year mark, and *after* he has built a good solid salable background.

But you should define *exactly what kind of job* you are shooting for at thirty-five and you should have a *specific idea of how much money* you want to be making at thirty-five.

Then you're in an intelligent position to lay out a plan and a schedule and to check up on yourself at least once a year to be sure you're following your plan and meeting your schedule.

And, once you've set your target at thirty-five, it is not too early to set up a tentative life plan beyond that age.

In doing so, you will find it helpful to divide your future into three main periods—up to thirty-five years of age, from thirty-five to fifty-five, and beyond fifty-five.

LIFE PLANNING CHART

Up to Age 35 *Objective #1*	From 35 to 55 *Objective #3*	Beyond 55 *Objective #5*
V Build a salable background, i.e., study in well recognized schools, do a good job for favorably known organizations. N The important point here A is whether you are acquiring *cashable* education and experience.	CASH IN on your salable experience from 35 to 55 or you probably never will. These are your PEAK EARNING YEARS and HOW MUCH MONEY you make IS IMPORTANT.	Set up your own business which you own, lock, stock, and barrel and over which you exercise complete control so that no one can fire you.

V
O
C
A
T
I
O
N
A
L

	Objective #2	Objective #4	Objective #6
A V O C A T I O N A L	Build STRONG SPONSORSHIP in your social and business relations. Continue to improve your job abilities through part-time reading and study programs, especially designed to fit your situation.	Avocationally, during these peak earning years, search for some interesting activity that will develop into your own business after 55.	Pursue some kind of hobby to give you a change of pace and to keep you from going stale.

☼ Some Model Designs for Achievement

Before you attempt to work out your own answers to the above six objectives, let's see how some other young men have worked out their personal designs for achievement. Just seeing these plans in print will stimulate you to think out your own plan.

Martin G. graduated from high school, spent two years in the Army, went to business school, and then took a job as bookkeeper for a small oil company. At twenty-four years of age, he charted his life plan as follows:

UP TO 35	FROM 35 TO 55	BEYOND 55
Vocation: Try to advance from bookkeeper to controller.	*Vocation:* Try to advance from controller to financial vice-president.	*Vocation:* Tax consultant to corporations and individuals.
Avocation: Study accounting at night school.	*Avocation:* Study special problems in corporation and personal taxation.	*Avocation:* Local politics.

Bill M. studied Business Administration for two years on the G.I. Bill and then decided to get married. His main interest was sales, and he got a job selling classified advertising, and then local display advertising, for a leading metropolitan daily newspaper. After spending four years on this job, he decided that he was more interested in national advertising than he was in local advertising, and at twenty-seven years of age he set up his program as follows:

UP TO 35	FROM 35 TO 55	BEYOND 55
Vocation:	*Vocation:*	*Vocation:*
Transfer to national advertising department of my newspaper and try to advance to job of assistant national advertising director.	Try to land job as national advertising director, either with my paper or some other paper.	Run small-town newspaper.
Avocation:	*Avocation:*	*Avocation:*
Take courses in advertising at local advertising club, and at local college.	Study small-town newspapers and save some money with a view to buying controlling interest in one.	Promote better schools, playgrounds and recreational facilities.

As soon as our old friend, Harry McM., got well started on his graduate study program for the doctorate, he decided that when he landed his Ph.D. at the age of thirty-two, he would accept a full-time teaching job in the graduate school of business where he was studying, and then he laid out his future as follows:

UP TO 35	FROM 35 TO 55	BEYOND 55
Vocation:	*Vocation:*	*Vocation:*
Finish my work for the doctorate and	Try to advance toward a full pro-	Marketing Consultant full-time when

take full-time teaching job, as an Instructor or Assistant Professor.	fessorship in the School of Business Administration.	I decide to retire as a teacher.
Avocation: Broaden my business contacts in the area with a view toward acting as part-time Marketing Consultant.	*Avocation:* Go after small consulting jobs in the area.	*Avocation:* Writing for business magazines, and maybe do a textbook on some phase of marketing.

When Thomas L. graduated as an industrial engineer, he took a job as an industrial engineering trainee with a big steel company. Three years later he was offered a job as engineering supervisor for a midwestern manufacturer and began to engineer some outstanding improvements. At twenty-eight, he laid out his plan as follows:

UP TO 35	FROM 35 TO 55	BEYOND 55
Vocation: Try to advance to assistant manager's job in my department or to a similar job in another good company.	*Vocation:* Try to advance to the job of Manager of Industrial Engineering.	*Vocation:* Own and operate a small manufacturing business.
Avocation: Become active in professional engineering associations and continue studies in industrial engineering.	*Avocation:* Be on the lookout for small manufacturers of gadgets and save some money with a view to either starting such a small manufacturing operation or buying a controlling interest in one later on.	*Avocation:* Work on new product ideas and inventions.

Each one of these young men may effect certain changes and revisions in these plans as the years go by. But at least they know where they're going, and so they are ever so much more likely to get there.

Now if you are a young man under thirty-five, you should be able to go ahead and chart your own course. Naturally, the age groups given above are merely rough approximations. How fast you progress is largely up to you. After all, many men build a salable background before they are thirty-five, and many are ready to go into business for themselves before they are fifty-five.

✿ If You're Thirty-five to Fifty-five

If you are a man between the ages of thirty-five to fifty-five, you are already in what should be your peak earning years. And if you enjoy your job and are making the kind of money you'd like to make, you're fortunate.

If you do not enjoy your job, however, or if you are not making as much money as you would like to, it's not too late to make the switch to the field that suits your requirements.

No matter what you've been doing, it's always possible to relate much of your past experience to the new field you prefer. In many cases, it isn't even necessary to take a temporary cut in income. And in some cases, it is possible for a person to boost his income when he makes the switch.

If you are wondering how you might change your field, you might go back to Chapter 8 and reread the case of Thomas D. and how he did it. And here are some more examples:

Harold B. was thirty-eight when he began to get fed up with his job as a salesman for a leading midwestern radio station. He was more interested in the field of general business administration and he began to send in suggestions for improving operations of the program production department and the general office, as well as the sales department. Within three years he got an appointment as staff assistant to the president. Now he is in line for the job of general manager.

Edward T., at forty-three years of age, was making around $30,000 a year as a customer's man in Wall Street. But he gradually came to hate his job. He liked people—all kinds of people—especially "the underdog." This fondness for people expressed itself in various avocational activities in the local Y.M.C.A. and Boy Scout movement. He was vice-president of his local college alumni association. His desires ran toward human service in a big way.

I suggested that he get into some phase of personnel administration.

He began to look around, talk to his best and most influential friends about the idea, and study the personnel field.

Within a year, he was offered a job as personnel manager by the president of a company whom he had served well as a customer's man, at the same money he was making in Wall Street. Two years later, he was appointed industrial relations director for the same company at a salary of $40,000 a year and given complete charge of the negotiations of all union contracts.

Recently, he was appointed to a top labor relations post in the national government in Washington.

✪ Avocational Preparation vs. Negative Thinking

The whole trouble is that as we grow older and acquire responsibilities, we grow more conservative, more opposed to change.

Now it's perfectly all right to be cautious, to figure

out every move in advance, and, if necessary, to effect a gradual shift of emphasis from your present job to your chosen field, preparing for the new job avocationally, so that you do not experience financial shock when you make the change. But it's a tragic mistake for you to fall victim to negative thinking and to assume that you must go on and on in a field you do not like, just because you are in it.

Avocationally, your most important objective between the ages of thirty-five and fifty-five is to prepare for the years beyond fifty-five. For this is the only way you can guard against the common fears which plague most men over fifty.

No matter how successful a man may be during his peak earning years, there comes a gradual realization that some day, sooner or later, maybe at fifty-five, maybe at sixty, maybe at sixty-five, he will be considered too old for his present job and will be replaced by someone younger. And as we have already pointed out, retirement is not the answer.

As former President Hoover said on his eighty-second birthday, "There is no joy to be had from retirement except some kind of productive work.

"Otherwise," he advised, "you degenerate into talking to everybody about your pains and pills and income tax. The other oldsters will want to talk about their own pains and pills and income tax. Any oldster who keeps at even part-time work has something worth talking about. He has a zest for the morning paper and his three meals a day. The point of all this is not to retire from work or you will shrivel up into a nuisance to all mankind.

"The problem is—find some other job where your skills and experience can get exercise—and America needs these skills and experience."

We have found only one satisfactory solution to this problem. And that is to devote part of your spare time, during your peak earning years, to a search for some avocational activity which promises to flower later in life into a vocational activity over which you can exercise complete control. And your chances of finding such an activity will be immeasurably improved if you take into account the following points:

1. It is best to select a business or activity in which you can use the abilities you have developed during your peak earning years. For example, we have very few cases in which a "city feller" made good as a farmer later in life. Our most successful cases are those where the person selected a *business which he already knew a lot about.*

2. Select a business or activity that you *can get excited about*—one that you believe in, one that satisfies your basic desires to perform a service or to do something worth while.

3. Select a business or activity that puts you into everyday relations with the *kind of people you enjoy.* This human relations factor is *tremendously important.*

4. Select a business or activity in which *age or experience are definite assets* rather than handicaps.

5. Select a business or activity which lends itself to *small-scale operations*—one that you can continue to *direct with ease* as long as you live. A big business is likely to become so complicated and burdensome that you might lose the essential control which is a primary requisite.

Men who intelligently prepare for the later years do a better job during their peak earning years because they lose all fear of growing old on the job. They have the satisfaction and assurance that comes from a real reason for existence and a real vision for the future later in life.

☆ If You're Over Fifty-five

If you're over fifty-five, and you're not your own boss, you have no time to lose. You should take immediate steps to prepare yourself to get into some kind of small agreeable business or activity of your own so that no one can fire you. If you don't, you may get an unpleasant shock any time from now on. And you're almost certain to get such a shock before many years have passed.

Of course, many men over fifty-five feel that they're pretty well set on their present job for five or even ten years. And they have a pension arrangement that pretty well takes care of their major needs from then on. So they are inclined to postpone any preparation for the later years.

This, of course, is a big mistake. For when the retirement day finally comes, they are unprepared to continue living an active and interesting life—whether they've got enough money or not.

If you still have any doubts about this, reread the case of Harvey H. in Chapter 5. And there, too, you will find a variety of examples of men who have found interesting activities over which they exercised control later in life.

You, too, can completely lose yourself in your own little business or activity—depending on what your interests are. For you, too, the later years can be a succession of interesting adventures.

∙∙

DESIGNS FOR WOMEN

∙∙

Many women marry and raise a family. Consequently, those women will find it helpful to divide their personal design for the future into three main periods:

➤➤1. The years before your marriage and immediately following your marriage—before the first baby arrives.

➤➤2. The years when you are busily engaged with the important job of raising your family.

➤➤3. The years after your family is raised and you need some new and compelling reason for existence.

Of course, any woman who remains single can plan her career in the very same way that a man does. And any woman who marries and who remains childless can also, if she wishes, pursue her favorite career either full-time or certainly part-time.

If you're in either of these categories, read and study the designs for men earlier in this chapter.

☼ *If You Want to Get Married and Raise a Family*

You remember Florence Q. When I first met her, she wanted to get married and she wanted to get into personnel work. It might be worth while for you to go back to Chapter 8 and reread the steps that she took to achieve these objectives.

Today, Florence is looking forward to having children and raising a family. But while she raises her family, she plans to keep in touch with the personnel world by subscribing to personnel journals, by keeping up her contacts with the people she knows in the field, and by taking an occasional course of study in order to keep up with developments in her field.

After her family is raised, Florence has tentatively decided that she will probably open a small employment agency for women somewhere in her home area, and avocationally act as a career counselor for women.

Similarly, if you are a young single woman, you can start out with your vocational desires and proceed to gain some salable background in your chosen field. Then, avocationally, you can get active in some local church or community affairs or take a course of study so that you will meet the kind of men you'd like to know, with a view toward marrying and raising a family. And, after your family is raised, you can return to your vocational pursuits.

✸ If You're a Housewife Who Is Raising a Family

If you are a housewife who is engaged in the important job of raising a family, you can pick up cues for your design for the future from the following cases.

First of all, it might be a good idea for you to reread the cases of Mary T. and Helen A. in Chapter 8.

Then there's Agnes R., who was an assistant fashion editor for a women's magazine before she was married and began raising her family. Now, with two children, a boy of six and a girl of eight, her hands are pretty full running a home, but she writes children's stories during her spare time and has sold some to the magazine she used to work for. Later, after her family is raised, she plans to spend most of her time writing magazine articles and children's books.

And Helen L., who was a school teacher before she

married, wrote and gave book reviews to various women's clubs in her section of West Virginia while her two girls were growing up. And now that her girls are of high school and college age, she holds a half-time position as executive secretary in a child's guidance center.

✿ *If You're a Woman Whose Family Is Raised*

If you're a woman whose family is raised, and you are looking for a new challenge that will keep you busy and make you feel important again, you might first of all re-read the case of Elsie van M. in Chapter 8.

Other women who are in the same situation and who are getting a big kick out of life are:

Ruth M., who teaches piano and voice.

Mary M., who runs a beauty supply business.

Elizabeth D., who operates six newspaper routes and who enjoys training boys to become "merchants."

Lucy L., who runs a book and gift shop.

Ivy D., who runs a small riding academy.

Ann D., who operates a nursery.

Ruth S., who raises and sells English and Irish setters.

MAN OR WOMAN—
NOW IT'S YOUR TURN

Now that you have seen how other men and women of various ages arrived at their own personal design for achievement, the time has come for you to do the same thing.

No matter who you are, how old you are, or what your present situation may be, you can start with what you want out of life just as these other men and women did, and build your own future.

It would be a good idea to get your notebook and pencil *now* and begin to write down not only your immediate objectives, but also your tentative ideas on long-range goals for the years to come.

Don't be afraid to put down dreams for the future that you are not entirely sure of as yet. For long-range plans are always subject to periodic review, revision, and refinement.

As the years roll by, you get to know yourself better. Your underlying desires become clearer, and you learn, by trial and error, the easiest ways to achieve your desires.

Naturally, you will want to keep improving your personal design for achievement as long as you live. And my first-hand experience with hundreds of men and women who are doing this right now has proved that the very best way to assure that *you* do so is to make a date with yourself once a year for an annual review.

✭ What To Do on Your Annual Date with Yourself

Once a year—say on your birthday, or on New Year's Day—sit down and review what has happened to you during the previous year. Find out whether you're meeting your schedule. Then detail specific and immediate goals for the coming year.

Put your annual review IN WRITING, including full comments on what you have done or failed to do during the past year. Write out any revisions in your general program. Make up a definite schedule covering what you WANT TO ACHIEVE DURING THE COMING YEAR and EXACTLY HOW YOU'RE GOING TO GET IT.

As time goes on, copies of these annual reviews become more and more valuable. You soon find out just how good a planner you are—whether you're inclined to be over-optimistic, over-pessimistic, or sound and realistic. You soon pick up your most common mistakes and learn how you can avoid them. You find that your plans become clearer and simpler every year.

Yes, these annual reviews of your life plan, reduced to writing, in due time become a vivid historical chronicle which reveals the evolution of your whole philosophy of life—what you believe is important, and specifically what you want to accomplish.

And once you know what you believe in and exactly what you want out of life—in terms of MONEY, LOVE, EGO FOOD, and HEALTH—your achievement of a full and well-balanced life is certain, for you'll find that you THINK, EAT, SLEEP, and DREAM the fulfillment of your desires.

And as long as you entertain bold dreams for the future, you will never grow old.

Life then becomes the exciting adventure it should be.

THE SUCCESS SYSTEM THAT NEVER FAILS

W. Clement Stone

Head of a multi-million dollar organization reveals money-making secrets which *anyone* can utilize for building a personal fortune! How successful you are is simple a matter of the right mental attitude and using the easy-to-follow principles in this book. *Includes:* Do Twice as Much in Half the Time; How to Get a Person to Listen to You; It Takes Less Work to Succeed Than to Fail; A Blueprint for Success; Hidden Channels of the Mind; How Wealth Is Made; Increased Wealth Through Giving; Foreign Credit Balances; A Test to Help You Discover Your Potential.

HOW TO DEVELOP A SUPER POWER MEMORY

Harry Lorayne

However poor you may *think* your memory is now, the author believes that you have a memory *10 to 20 times more powerful than you realize!* He maintains that your memory is working at a tiny fraction of its true power today — because *you simply don't know the right way to feed it facts!* Because you don't know the right way to take names and faces and anything else you want to remember — *and burn them into your memory so vividly that you can never forget them!* The most practical, lucid and effective memory-training book ever published.